Academic Life

STUDIES IN PHILOSOPHY, CULTURE AND CONTEMPORARY SOCIETY

Edited by Bogusław Paź

VOLUME 44

Zbigniew Drozdowicz

Academic Life

My Point of View

Translated by Szymon Nowak

PETER LANG
Berlin · Bruxelles · Chennai · Lausanne · New York · Oxford

Bibliographic Information published by the Deutsche Nationalbibliothek
The Deutsche Nationalbibliothek lists this publication in the Deutsche Nationalbibliografie; detailed bibliographic data is available online at http://dnb.d-nb.de.

Library of Congress Control Number: 2025024189

Cover image courtesy of Bartosz Wozniak.
The cover depicts a work of art, an installation of Piotr Tetlak.

The publication has been financially supported by the Centre for Interdisciplinary Research in Poznan. Poland.

ISSN 2196-0151
ISBN 978-3-631-93768-6 (Print)
ISBN 978-3-631-93769-3 (ePDF)
ISBN 978-3-631-94132-4 (ePUB)
DOI 10.3726/b23088

Published by Peter Lang GmbH, Berlin (Germany)

info@peterlang.com

This publication has been peer reviewed.

www.peterlang.com

Table of Contents

From the Author

In this volume, I share some of the observations and reflections that arose while I navigated the academic environment in the course of a long journey from being a student at the Adam Mickiewicz University (AMU) in Poznań to a full professor in the field of Humanities, in the discipline of Philosophy. That makes well over 50 years all told: I started studying history in 1968, while my full-time employment at this university concluded as the academic year 2023/24 came to an end. Much happened during that time, not only in my academic life; my private life and the political life of the country where I was born and where I worked saw many changes as well. If I had to recapitulate the events relating to my academic life in as few words as possible, I would say that I gained an independence of thought that allows me to look at its past and present with a certain distance. This does not mean, however, that I look at it indifferently. My statements in this book as well as in many earlier publications of mine attest to the contrary. Naturally, what arouses my most profound interest and sentiments are the issues surrounding the realities of academic life in Poland. Even so, they are not the only ones, because never has that life functioned in isolation from the developments abroad, predominantly in the East until the turn of 1989 and in the West afterwards. I addressed those earlier relations and affiliations more extensively in periodicals such as *Forum Akademickie* and *Nauka. Kwartalnik PAN* and discussed the later both in those magazines and in several monographs. This volume includes a selection of my previous texts published there, though there are few which do not contain significant revisions and additions. A fair number, on the other hand, have never been published before. Am I thoroughly objective in my observations? This I cannot say. Nonetheless, I have at least tried to temper my subjective point of view enough to avoid the accusation of not knowing what I am talking about. Obviously, it is not for me to judge whether my efforts in that respect have been successful. I might just add that even where I opt for a humorous tone, I take the issues at hand very seriously. Ultimately, however, this book has not been intended as a scientific treatise, but rather as a collection of essays which leave room for a certain liberty of expression.

World-class and provincialism in science

For many a scientist, the desire for their research to achieve international status motivates them to be more active professionally. The problem is that there has never been a single standard of world-class and, moreover, the standards which apply in certain scientific disciplines are not completely compatible with others. On top of it, within the same discipline, one may meet the standards of world-classness in one respect but not in another and effectively practice a peculiar provincialism. Despite the complexity, one can still identify at least some traits of that worldliness and provincialism alike.

World-class science

This kind of science is heard about when, for instance, prestigious awards are given for discoveries whose significance only a few understand. In fact, it is not necessary for many to understand. It suffices that they can be appraised and appreciated by the experts who decide whether an accolade should be awarded. Naturally, they too can be wrong and sometimes they are, while person also have substantial scientific achievement but for various reasons have not received such honours may even think that this happens too often. Such thinking may or may not be indicative of provincialism. The same applies to the various rankings of universities where research is conducted and students educated. They differ and none of them can be said to account for everything that is best about such institutions with mathematical accuracy. However, those which happen to be taken fairly seriously in the academic milieu – like the Shanghai Ranking – rely on similar criteria, such as the number of Nobel Prize winners among the graduates and faculty, or the number of research projects carried out by international research teams, while their funding is comparable to the means allocated by large industrial corporations for their undertakings. Even if other criteria were adopted, the list of world science usually features the same academic and research centres, primarily American (such as Harvard University or the Massachusetts Institute of Technology) but several European universities are not far behind (such as Cambridge and Oxford). All that has been said here about world science is a well-known fact, reiterated not only on those occasions when one wants to 'give to Caesar what belongs to Caesar's', but also to suggest models to follow for those who still lack something to be able to ascend that 'throne'.

A few words also due regarding the scholars who made significant contributions to science. Not infrequently, their professional and private lives are no big secret, as plenty of testimonial literature has been devoted to the topic (for those interested, I recommend the memoirs of Jane Hawking, Stephen Hawking's first wife). However, it is relatively seldom read, which is a shame, because one would at least be more cautious in formulating generalisations about individuals whose achievements are monumental, but who could hardly be included among the saints. Still, I am not going to discuss the sins – venial or otherwise – of anyone; instead, I will draw on the recollections of Andrzej Walicki (published in *Przegląd Filozoficzny* no. 1/2014) from his time working at All Souls College, Oxford University. It clearly follows from his account that it was not considered good manners among the scholars employed there to emphasise at every turn what they themselves had published or underscore that information about their achievements may be found in the references to their publications contained in the studies of their friends and subordinates (in Oxford, this is considered a 'parvenu trait'). Instead, one should maintain a certain distance towards oneself and one's otherwise worldly company, manifesting in the annual celebration of 'drunkard's day' (when one simply has to 'get sloshed'). In 1986, A. Walicki was awarded a funded professorship in History of Ideas (O'Neil Family Chair) at the Department of History, Catholic University of Notre Dame in Indiana (US). The long-standing president of that university – a formally Catholic institution with ecumenical curriculum – was Father Theodore M. Hesburgh, an outstanding American educational activist, recipient of the highest state honours for his fight for human rights and his vigorous appeals to the public concerning the threat of nuclear disaster. He sought to make Notre Dame 'a great Catholic university while stressing that it would be a *university*, not a religious establishment'. In Poland, some Catholic university rectors could be found who would readily subscribe to such a notion. And yet, it would be more difficult to find those willing to concur that a university can be Catholic but does not have to be religious.

Provincial science

It is not that every form of provincialism has to connote negatively, since much depends on the historical and cultural context. For example, in France, everything outside Paris has been considered provincial for centuries, including the universities whose achievement in terms of science and academic education is by no means insignificant. As globalisation intensifies, provincialism (also known as regionalism) can and often does appear to be a healthy mode of safeguarding one's cultural identity against those who would like to 'dress' that culture in the same or a very similar suit to the one tailored in another part of the world (often in America). The same is or at least can be true in science, notably in those disciplines which rely on research into local cultures. Still, it must be noted that in countries such as England or France, these disciplines do not qualify as *science*, but as literature *(lettres)*, though international achievements are expected to be drawn upon even there. In the age of open borders and online communication one can engage in scientific work at a provincial centre and yet conduct world-class research. However, one must be willing and able to use such opportunities. Those who can use the latter, but do not wish to or are unable to take advantage of the former, practice a kind of substitute for world-classness. I am thinking, among others, about those who believe that each result of scientific research can and should be converted into points that accurately reflect the standing of their author in the ranking of scientists. Even in the United States, the country where the epidemic of pointosis and Hirsch indexomania began – there are universities where this is not reduced to 'citability'. The aforementioned A. Walicki writes that at the University of Notre Dame, points were awarded not only for publications, but also for 'good working conditions, including the remunerations and scholarships, for the composition of the student body (with a premium for multiraciality and maximum number of female students), as well as student satisfaction with teaching, of course. (…) "Citability", on the other hand, was rightly approached with a pinch of salt, while an excessive number of publications was considered (as in Australia) suspicious …' In 1981–1986, A. Walicki was employed as an independent researcher at the Department of the History of Ideas at the Australian University in Canberra, where his colleagues included, for example, 'the world-renowned historian of philosophy John Passmore, and political philosophy flourished at the Department of Philosophy; one of its representatives, Philip Petit, became the world's leading theorist of 'republicanism', which has earned the ANU one of the leading positions in the international ranking of philosophy it enjoys today'.

The pointosis and Hirsch indexomania rampant in our country bears at least outward appearances of world-classness. On the other hand, it would be difficult to find them in such manifestations of scientific provincialism as engaging solely with local problems, while the results of such research are communicated primarily to add another item to the list of one's publications. Nor can they be easily found in the attempts to tackle major issues that, essentially, have already been solved by others. One has to be aware of this, but that requires familiarity with international literature and the ability to use research methods whose effectiveness has repeatedly been demonstrated by various scientists. Needless to say, command of foreign language skills is indispensable in that regard. Even so, it may not be enough without direct interaction with major scientists, who could share much about the advantages, disadvantages and limitations of the research methods they employ. There are, of course, various ways for such contacts to be established. One of the most popular is to participate in scholarly life by attending international conferences and having one's findings discussed. And yet, such participation may also serve as a peculiar 'cover' for scientific provincialism. After all, quite a few important and serious scientific conferences see both world-class and provincial papers, whether in terms of the issue one investigates, or the manner in which it is handled and presented. Fellowships and guest lectures represent a less popular form of participation in international academic life, but they are effective only if they take place at significant academic centres and do not consist in 'dead souling' there (which is how a stay without actual participation in the academic life of that centre could be called).

Questions and suggestions

The most fundamental question is not the Hamletic 'to be or not to be' world-class in science. It is fairly obvious that it is better to be such a scholar rather than not to. The question, however, is in what respects it is worthwhile and appropriate to be one, so as to enter the 'salons' of world science without feeling insecure or risking ridicule. Some will certainly claim that fluency in English is essential. I would suggest that they read the biographies of those non-English-speaking scientists who, at least at the beginning of their international careers, struggled seriously with the language (if interested, do read *Niels Bohr's Times* by A. Pais). Obviously, in a country as attached to its traditions as England, it is better to know English than not to, and even better to speak it with an Oxford accent. However, in a country like France, it is advisable to speak French and, if possible, with a Parisian accent. What I am trying to say is that a reasonable command of foreign languages may be helpful at such academic 'salons', but it does not suffice to be recognised as a fully-fledged participant of that worldly life.

Another question concerns those people who have been present at many 'salons' of the kind and know the rules which apply there, and yet constantly violate them – for example, by publishing numerous scientific monographs (according to A. Walicki, three in an entire scientific career are considered the limit of decency in the USA) and, on top of that, producing numerous papers only to publicly flaunt that output, adding insult to injury. Regrettably, nobody is perfect. But is it not suspicious and even annoying that some scientists depart so far from the average publication rate in their field that their immediate and broader milieu finds it difficult to answer how they do it and why they do it? Perhaps they are trying to hide some of their latent insecurities in this manner or simply want to upset us. I am joking, of course, but only a bit. In my academic environment, I did come across such scientifically overactive persons (although they were not numerous), as well as heard similar opinions voiced (of which there were more). They were often accompanied by attempts to denigrate the scholarly achievements of those overactive individuals.

Perhaps a little self-reflection is due. If we adopt the world-classness criterion of no more than a few scientific monographs during one's entire scientific career, then I am one of the provincials. Unfortunately, my monograph count is much higher, only to be far surpassed by the number of papers which, worse still, increases year by year (being alarmingly close to 600 at present). I cannot find any convincing justification for that breach of the community's custom. I am certainly not interested in reaching another milestone in my academic career (the last of my major promotions was more than 25 years ago). Nor am I interested in seeking the recognition of experts who review research projects in various competitions (as they effectively discouraged me from doing so a decade ago). I could say that I consider writing and publishing to be my professional duty and even admit that it comes relatively easy to me. However, can such an excuse be taken seriously? What is worse, it might offend those who work in the same profession but are able to maintain a far greater restraint in presenting the outcomes of their inquiries. At any rate, my provincialism will bring no blush of shame to my cheeks.

The limits of academic freedoms

Academic freedoms are among the values written into the statutes of universities since the first ones were founded, being invoked whenever external forces tried to interfere with their research and educational curricula. The problem is that there have always been limits to these freedoms, boundaries that either cannot or should not be crossed.

Limits of the freedom of speech

This limit is relatively the most difficult to demarcate. What constitutes an expression of this freedom for some violates some 'sanctity' – with or without quotation marks – for others, especially at those universities whose character had or has a religious element to it. Naturally, one can draw on such general provisions as those found, for instance, in the French *Declaration of the Rights of Man and of the Citizen* of 1789, which asserts that this freedom is circumscribed by the freedom of another person and citizen. However, it soon became apparent that such statutes are so general as to be interpreted in various ways and 'bent' to the needs of the current powerholder. Things turned even worse later on, especially in those countries whose banners proclaimed the liberation of the urban and rural working masses from injustice, but which in practice catered to the needs of a relatively small group of politicians and ideologists. One could also cite those university traditions that translated into the most substantial and worthwhile contributions to science and formation of students. Indeed, there have been such periods and such universities, but they represented a decided minority all the same.

Even those that may be counted among the notable exceptions also witnessed periods in their history that they would rather forget. However, they tend to be reminded of the past by their former students, such as Edward Gibbon – graduate from the Magdalene College at Oxford – who said of his academic teachers that 'from the toil of reading or thinking or writing they had absolved their conscience. Their conversation stagnated in a round of college business, Tory politics, personal stories and private scandal; their dull and deep potations excused the brisk intemperance of youth'. However, he studied there for a short time (from 1752 to 1753), having been expelled from the university after converting from Anglicanism to Catholicism. Still, he made his mark in the history of English culture, not so much with the autobiography an excerpt from which is quoted here, but with the *History of the Decline and Fall of the Roman Empire* in six volumes (the first of which was published in 1776). Yet, these are no grounds to say that even a university in such a state of decline as Oxford at that time is capable of producing such an outstanding historian, since Gibbon owed his academic education primarily to the University of Lausanne. I mention that English historian and politician because his autobiography offers a good starting point for discussing the limits of a freedom of speech known as the 'good name of the university'.

Such a problem would also arise with other scholars, including A. Einstein. In *The Private Life of Albert Einstein*, R. Highfield and P. Carter state that the scientist was accepted at the Zurich Polytechnic only on his second attempt and, once he had graduated, he opined in a letter to his wife Mileva (Marić) that the Polytechnic director who rejected his first application 'taught clearly but too superficially'. Obviously, this is not the kind of 'fouling' of one's academic nest as was the case with Gibbon. However, almost every one of Einstein's opinions was later read by all kinds of curious individuals and reproduced not only by those who studied somewhere and developed their own view on the realities of academic life, but also by those who were merely outside observers of that life and possibly looked for an excuse to give the university gates a 'wide berth'. More than a few of the accounts and assessments in Einstein's biography offer ample grounds for debating freedom of speech where it concerns the private life of scientists. Merely for the sake of example, let us quote the above authors, who claim that during his studies Einstein 'was already very absent-minded – forever forgetting his keys or umbrella, or leaving behind his nightshirt and wash things when he went home in the holidays'.

The limits of financial freedom

Apparently, gentlemen do not talk about money. True, perhaps, for those who have so much that they would not be able spend it in their lifetime. Scholars, on the other hand, are unlikely to have ever belonged to this group. Obviously, there are some who have enough money to lead a relatively comfortable private life and receive sufficient funds in their professional life to carry out even expensive research. However, they are definitely few. The majority have to put in substantial effort to obtain the funds and then spend it so that everything may be accounted for and then, possibly, apply for more. However, academic centres which can boast the most significant achievements in scientific research and its practical implementation dispose of financial means that the centres working their way up the ladder can only dream of. It is no coincidence that American universities have occupied the top spots in the prestigious Shanghai Ranking for years. Harvard University has the largest budget, which according to Forbes exceeds $32 billion. Further twenty-two universities in the US are considered 'rich' as well. In total, they have approximately $223 billion to spend. However, there are about 4,000 higher education institutions in the United States and, even if they do not struggle to make ends meet, they have to appreciate every student who is able to pay the costs of studying there.

In most European countries, one studies at the taxpayers' expense. Those which qualify as affluent have not so much very wealthy universities as financial managers who see to it that there is enough for both research and education. Naturally, such managers are not found only at university level. Currently, Poland does not count among the rich countries, as it merely tries to catch up with the West in terms of wealth. Hence the long-standing notion of academic poverty. Admittedly, funds allocated to research and development increased from 0.8% of GDP in 2016 to 1.65% in 2023, but this is still a far cry from the 3%+ earmarked by countries such as Sweden, Austria and Germany. The year 2024 saw major change in Polish policies. Even the election manifesto of the coalition that ultimately came to power included a commitment to increase the salaries of all teachers – including university instructors – by 30% and the remunerations of support and administrative staff by 20%. This actually ensued, being one of the most significant steps towards improving the living standard of those professional groups. Although the subsidy for universities to sustain their teaching and research potential was also increased in 2024, it clearly failed to match the actual rise in the costs involved, manifesting – among other things – in the liquidity issues that many of those institutions faced, the leading universities included. It is likely that many frantically looked for additional revenue and savings, as well as 'cut' whatever and whoever can be cut without risking major protests from the university community. Will 2025 be better financially? That remains to be seen.

For the time being, it is vital not to exceed the financial limits at universities and other research units. Things may be different in practice, though. Several years ago, I was the chair of the Senate's budget and finance committee at the Adam Mickiewicz University. The university's budget balanced (otherwise it would have faced an audit and a recovery scheme in which financial cuts would have been a priority). Still, it required certain 'acrobatics' which meant shifting funds from financially sound university units to those which were thoroughly unable to generate means to maintain their infrastructure and staff. In some cases, their establishment was due to erroneous calculations of the previous university authorities, and in others it had to be attributed to the overambitious rectors who, managing university funds, presumed that their successors would somehow manage. Consequently, the university took over such branches which had neither the adequate academic personnel nor the people interested in studying there – at the time when 'money followed the student'. One would build high-maintenance facilities whose size, albeit impressive, does not reflect the quality of research conducted there. To say that the financial capabilities of the university were exceeded there is an understatement. At the time, those who held the rector's office went way beyond the limits of both imagination and responsibility with which they had been entrusted.

The so-called 'sacred cows'

It is likely that some will find such strong a term inapplicable in academic polemics. One could speak of 'untouchables' instead, but it would mean the same. On the other hand, it fails to sufficiently convey the functioning of those who not only consider themselves superior to their fellow academics but also find others who confirm them in that belief. Either way, such people have found in this life and come in several different 'subspecies'.

The first includes individuals who express views that are in line with their deepest convictions but contrary to the current state of knowledge. And if they have some institutional support and a scientific degree, they can pass as authorities. Here, I speak not only of various anti-vaxxers, but also of the medical professionals who, pleading the conscience clause, refuse to perform medical procedures that can save health and, in extreme cases, life. A colleague of mine – a professor with long academic experience – calls them 'flat-earthers'. The harmfulness of such 'sacred cows' is often demonstrated not only in the media but also in serious academic presentations, but they seem to be doing well for the time being and even have the ability to proliferate at an astonishing rate. It must also be said that they do not generally have an easy life in higher education institutions.

It is easier for those who talk such nonsense in class that even moderately intelligent students grow doubtful. However, if they complain to the dean, the inept lecturers can invoke the section of the Great Charter of European Universities, which states that 'freedom in research and training is the fundamental principle of university life, and governments and universities, each as far as in them lies, must ensure respect for this fundamental requirement'. One could obviously attempt to verify whether the students' complaint is justified. I know a case of an institute deputy director for student affairs who tried to find out peeping through a keyhole what was said in such classes and whether they even took place. Apparently, they did, but what was being said was impossible to establish. However, no remedial steps could be taken because the matter concerned a full professor.

The relatively largest subgroup of the 'sacred cows' is composed of academics who still have some teaching duties but have long since forgotten about engaging in any research, even though they hold positions of both researcher and instructor and have their work reviewed by periodic evaluation committees at each faculty. As dean, I chaired such a committee for eight years. The assessment was based on periodic evaluation surveys that had to be completed by the person concerned and signed by their immediate superiors, followed by an interview before the committee. Demonstrating any scientific achievement was quite a challenge for them, while convincing the committee members that their assessment should be positive or at least conditionally positive proved even more difficult. It did happen, however, that those persons had their 'defence attorney' in the committee, capable of 'spinning something out of nothing' where their achievement was concerned. If, on the other hand, the assessment was negative, they usually petitioned the appeals committee, which sometimes ruled in their favour. In those appeals, they would either cite difficult family situation or their health. If, on top of that, the person was close to retirement, they had even greater chance of succeeding. Ultimately, they would scrape through yet another periodic evaluation. Here, the academic status of such a person played the paramount role. It was difficult not to recognise their arguments if that person held a postdoctoral degree. And whenever full professor was involved, they did not even have to make special efforts to argue their right to be an academic and remain among the academics. After all, no university has a surplus of such professors, while those who are there should be looked after rather than accused of being scientifically inactive.

Creating academic greats

In the academic milieu, there are greats who epitomise 'greatness' in the eyes of more than a few of its members. There are also those who may seldom be recognised but must be reckoned with in the academic lives of many. From time to time, though, the individuals who rise to the academic limelight make one wonder how they got there. However, they are a testament to one of the possible academic scenarios by means of such great figures are forged.

Institutional creation

This mode of creation has a long tradition, as it dates back to the distant past when the first universities were founded, that is, in the late eleventh and the early twelfth century. At that time, they were under ecclesiastic oversight and anyone who aspired to academic greatness would inevitably take what the Church superiors had to say about him on board. Although universities had their autonomy (meaning they were entitled to …), it did not go so far as to allow one to be an academic scholar and lecturer if, besides compliance with the conscience clause, they opted for a way of thinking that contradicted the teachings of the Church. Those scholars on whom it dawned at some point that something was wrong with those teachings and began to put amendments forward, soon found out that it was the case. Naturally, they were aware that the church authority might not like the suggestions and many of such innovators preferred to leave them 'in the drawer' for the sake of peace of mind – at least until they passed away and could no longer be harmed, by anything or anybody save God (if he indeed existed and took interest in the 'novelty seekers'). Such examples are numerous.

One of them was Isaac Newton. *A Portrait of Isaac Newton*, the biography by Frank E. Manuel, includes a chapter entitled *Prophecy and History*, according to which 'four volumes, about a thousand folios, chiefly on chronology and theology' were discovered the second half of the twentieth century. Let me remind you that the scholar was a Trinity College professor at Cambridge, while those documents show that he was seriously doubtful about the existence of the Holy Trinity. He probably did not expect that his reflections would elevate him to the altars. On the other hand, it is doubtless that he hoped for the findings he presented in *Mathematical Principles of Natural Philosophy* (first published in 1687) to make him a saint in science. And they did. Obviously, the treatise – written in mathematical language – is not a read for everyone. However, those who decided to pick the volume up, read and understand it found that it was a brilliant work by a genius like no other before him. Such a view is expressed, for example, in Albert Einstein's and Leopold Infeld's *The Evolution of Physics*. According to the authors, Newton had carried out a scientific 'assault' on the errors that many scholars continued to repeat for centuries by (the 'riddle of colour' being only one of those). One might ask: where is institutionalism in all of this? The thing is, it is there. As Peter L. Berger and Thomas Luckmann argue in *The Social Construction of Reality*, institutions are not confined to various churches and universities; all individuals capable of 'coupling' different spheres of reality qualify as institutions as well. Those 'couplers' can and often do include the 'intersubjectively comprehensible and binding linguistic forms of communication, as well as types of behaviour with which different people can identify, and a division of roles that comprises such typifications and embodies the institutional order'. In each case, 'institutionalisation occurs whenever there is a reciprocal typification of habitualised actions by types of actors. Put differently, any such typification is an institution. [...] They are available to all the members of the particular social group in question, and the institution itself typifies individual actors as well as individual actions'. Perhaps this is phrased a little too intricately. So, to put it simply: any such scholar who enjoys widespread interest and well-deserved recognition, at least among those who are well versed in scientific problems and solutions, may also be considered an institution. Newton was such an institution at the turn eighteenth century, followed by the aforementioned Einstein in the twentieth century.

Creation through awards and honours

In the academic community, the Nobel Prize is considered the 'top-of-the-line' accolade. The problem is that it was established only in 1901, and it is conferred in a few selected fields of science. The scholarly pursuits at the academia include many disciplines that do not fall under any of the categories in which the prize is awarded. In effect, Nobel Prize laureates make up only a small fraction of those involved in scientific research, even though some of them achieve results that are widely recognised around the world. Naturally, they can also seek other prestigious accolades, such as the Albert Einstein World Award of Science, given annually by the World Cultural Council since 1990 (though it is not quite the same as the Nobel Prize, of course). In the academic community, there is also a category of those who are said to have 'narrowly missed winning the Nobel Prize' (some of whom I have met during my academic career), but again, they are relatively few. On the other hand, there is no shortage of individuals who have received some kind of award and boast it not only in front of their family, but also in front of those who are not always well aware of its rank in the academic hierarchy.

Prize-wise, some remarks need to be made about the academic realities in Poland. For several years now, the awards conferred by the institutions which have obtained the status of 'research universities' are considered the most prestigious. This is not to say that other universities do not engage in scientific research, only that some carry it out at the relatively highest level. An international team of experts has selected ten such universities and identified ten others for 'the waiting room' until the next parameterisation (indeed, some were very close to making the top ten). This is no trifling matter, as it entails the allocation of additional ministerial funds for research and development. The financial benefits also include awards from the Prime Minister, the Minister of Science and the Rector for outstanding scientific, teaching and organisational achievement, with the scholarly accomplishment crowning the academic hierarchy. However, the rector's awards are nothing to be sniffed at either, especially the first-degree prize for scientific achievement. Although awarded annually, relatively few scientists receive them. More academics are given second-degree rector's awards, while the recipients of the third-degree accolades are the most numerous group. I have worked at the university for over 50 years, but I am unable to answer the following question convincingly: what are the measures applied to gauge the 'outstandingness'? It clearly is something more than just having one's work published in the world's most prestigious journals (after all, such publications are fewer than the awards). In any case, recipients of the superior university prizes are usually invited to a formal meeting with the institution' authorities and get to hear a few kind words about their achievements. How those achievements and the award are viewed by those who have not been thus honoured depends not only on their self-criticism (or lack thereof), but also on the objectivity with which the academic accomplishment are assessed by persons who apply for (usually deans or directors of various organisational units within the university) and grant the awards. Obviously, the decision ultimately rests with the rectors and their most trusted advisors. Still, those members of the academic community who win second- or third-degree prizes may also feel a sense of satisfaction since, first, even smaller amounts of money do boost their household budgets, and second, because there are many who have not received any prize at all.

The accolades given by students to their lecturers are a separate category. At my university, one of the most prestigious awards of the kind is the *Praeceptor Laureatus*, given to lecturers every year based on the results of student surveys. I do not wish to underestimate its importance, especially when it goes to academics who successfully combine their teaching and research duties. You come across such individuals, but not too frequently. More often, the teacher thus distinguished does fairly average research or even none at all, since they are employed in a teaching position and research is not a part of their duties. Whether it is possible to be a very good academic teacher without doing any research remains a debatable issue. I would not expect students to offer a convincing answer in that respect. The latter are often guided by the criteria which evince their need to study in a relatively pleasant fashion and to complete the successive stages of their studies with little hassle, which can hardly be reconciled with the strict knowledge requirements imposed by lecturers at exams.

'The third power'

I put the above term in quotation marks not so much because it is a kind of 'power without force', but mainly because I (not being alone in that sentiment) have serious misgivings about the making of academic grace through it. However, it is very real. It is the power of the bibliometrists and the bibliometric indices they use, which to some constitute an academic pathology and the most reliable marker of academic greatness to others. Moreover, it seems that the position of the former is weakening while the latter are growing in strength. This should be attributed to both the ability mastered by the bibliometrists (and the followers of their faith) to obtain a relatively high Hirsch index (which has become nearly God-like for some), and the support of ministerial authorities for their actions. I have discussed these bibliometrists and bibliometrics more extensively in the Polish Academy of Sciences quarterly *Nauka*, no. 2/2019. I will therefore only recall that this 'third power' in the academic community emerged relatively recently (its beginnings date to the late 1960s when Alan Pritchard and Robert A. Faithorne developed and applied statistical methods to determine the popularity of publications) and – at least in its original intention – it looked fairly innocent (having been designed mainly for library purposes). However, it soon 'grew' an academic 'plumage', manifesting not only in newspeak such as Impact Factor or alternative metrics, but in its inclusion among the criteria of academic achievement that are taken into account whenever academic promotions and prestigious research grants are applied for. As it stands today, the bibliometrists may not have yet become the highest authority on academic greatness, but at least they feel entitled to 'boss around' those whose Hirsch index is not particularly high for various reasons. Consider, for instance, the computation of the index for all candidates for the Council for Scientific Excellence (about 30% of whom scored zero) and the fact of it being posted on Emanuel Kulczycki's Facebook page. Perhaps there is more to this than just ridiculing the null-scorers. Either way, it is quite a bold move. The only question is whether it is prudent enough to do Polish science any good? As a consolation to those who did not notch up a high H in the humanities and social sciences, I would say that they are in quite good company, being among the scholars with superior contributions in the history of Polish culture. On the other hand, if I were in the shoes of the natural scientists whose Hirsch index equals or exceeds the level seen with Nobel Prize winners, I would hold on with the white tie for the award ceremony, because someone might find that this does not translate into world-class achievement.

What about myself?

Even if that question is a bit tongue-in-cheek, the answer is not meant in jest. I would not want to pick on those who, for reasons known only to themselves, did not award me any of the academic honours (many an academic has probably encountered such people). Instead, I wish to say a few words about the distinctions that I or my discipline have received. For those, I do not need to apologise to anyone, I believe. First of all, the results of parameterisation of the field as part of which I have submitted with my publications. It seems to be doing very well, having been recognised in the highest category (A+) in 2023. As regards the professorship, it is not too shabby, as I was conferred the title at the age of 44 (and it was not given to me on credit). With respect to rector's awards, it is more than good, as there were numerous, in various categories at that. Things are much less impressive in terms of honourable and teaching distinctions, because despite such a long life at the academia, none have come my way. The accolade I value the most was the extension of my employment at the university until I was 75 (by law, I should have been sent into retirement 10 years earlier). What did I do to deserve this? The answer is known to those rectors who agreed for me to work so long at the university (it turns out that I worked there for more than half a century).

Academic masters and teachers

Even those who have not attended any university may be familiar with the statement attributed to the ancient philosopher Heraclitus of Ephesus: *panta rhei* (everything changes, everything flows). Meanwhile, those with academic background can at least partially answer why things change and in where such changes are heading. However, I will go a little further beyond this somewhat philosophical reflection and try to explore how the role of masters and teachers has transformed in the academic environment.

The masters and teachers of the past

Philosopher will find it relatively easy to name them; not only were they numerous, but also – even above all – the relationship between the master and teacher and their students had largely been forged by ancient philosophers and later adopted into academic culture. Socrates is often considered the master and teacher of all philosophers who came after. Although he did not write anything himself, much was written about him by those who followed his recommendations and those who questioned them. In short, the resulting picture is not uniform. It is currently believed that what is said about a person is less important than the fact of being talked about as such. Later on, the Middle Ages saw masters who successfully competed with philosophers. Although they 'entered the race' in a different discipline, that is, theology, but it was and still is regarded an academic one. One of those great masters was Thomas Aquinas. During his studies at the University of Paris, he was ridiculed because of his obesity (he was even called 'the buffalo').

However, after he had obtained the degree of *magister* (master's), he went on to write theological treatises that earned him sainthood and recognition as a Doctor of the Catholic Church. Moreover, Aquinas also found many such students and followers that may still be readily found at Catholic universities, such as the Catholic University of Lublin in Poland.

An interesting example of a more recent master and teacher is Galileo Galilei. He went down in history not only for his scientific achievements, but also for the trial before the Inquisition, which lasted several years and ended with Galileo being forced to recant his Copernican view of the 'world system'. His *Dialogue Concerning the Two Chief World Systems, Ptolemaic and Copernican*, shows how masterfully he conceptualised them and how convincingly he argued for Copernicus' views. However, prior to becoming a master himself, Galileo was a diligent student of the Copernican 'school' and admired his master for his trust in the intellect and the ability to use it to 'rise above the changing evidence of the senses'. Galileo's biographer, James Reston Jr, portrays him as a masterful preceptor (Galileo was a lecturer in mathematics and astronomy at the University of Padua) who skilfully employed a wide range of communicative devices to get through to his students (for instance, 'he played first, like any good teacher, to the emotions of the audience and then appealed to knowledge over superstition'). He also demonstrated considerable mastery during the aforementioned trial. After all, it was quite an art to be 'for' and even 'against' for so many years. Even when the judges had realised that Galileo was essentially against the geocentric theory upheld by the Church and subscribed to Copernicus' theory, and that his formal declarations could not be taken too seriously, he is reported to have said on leaving the courtroom: 'And yet it moves' (meaning the motion of the Earth around the Sun, not the opposite).

In still less distant times, that is, in the nineteenth and twentieth century, epoch-making discoveries were made in science, and pioneering theories were formulated in disciplines in, for example, evolutionary biology and theoretical physics, by scholars such as Charles Darwin and Albert Einstein. What distinguished one from the other was not just the discipline, but also the fact that the former did not feel very confident in the academic environment (and never became a professor), whereas the latter – on the contrary – sought employment and was hired at various universities (the last of which was the prestigious Princeton University). Already as an academic professor, Einstein would engage in serious polemics with other academic professors who did not share his views. One of the most notorious was his dispute about the realness of light quanta with the Cambridge professor Niels Bohr. In the 1920s, Einstein began to function as the kind of master of whom practically anyone could ask a question and receive a correct answer. It must be noted that some of his answers gained worldwide fame, like the iconic 'God does not play dice', for example. His biographers, R. Highfield and P. Carter, wrote that 'Einstein became a media sage, courted the world over'. In fact, the authors attribute some blame for his becoming 'omniscient' to the international media. The weaknesses of that scholar aside, he was a world-class master and teacher, not only for those students who listened to his university lectures, but also for the subsequent generations of scholars.

The domestic realities

It is not true that Polish science has had no masters and teachers who could compete with their foreign counterparts. They may be found both in the more distant past, but also in fairly recent times, and Maria Curie-Skłodowska is not the only one. Incidentally, it may be worthwhile to recall that even A. Einstein was inclined to recognise her as a master in science (except that he treated her as a kind of 'accident at scientific work'). However, we do not abound in masters and teachers as might be inferred from the obituaries of late professors or the funeral eulogies of their disciples and colleagues. Just to be clear, I have no intention of either denigrating the importance of such speeches or attempting to enumerate Polish scholars who deserve to be called masters (both would find multiple opponents, no doubt). However, I would like to share a few remarks about the masters in the discipline that is closest to me, that is, philosophy.

Let me draw at this point on the philosopher Kazimierz Twardowski, the founder of the Lvov-Warsaw school. His students and the continuators of the school remember him not so much as an outstanding philosopher, but as a superb academic teacher whose lectures drew crowds of students. Both students and philosophers who later rose to some eminence valued Twardowski for his punctuality, ingenuous choice of topics and readings, and precision with which he formulated judgements and opinions. One of his pupils, Tadeusz Kotarbiński, wrote somewhat jokingly that he would 'strike terror into hearts', being an 'imperious man that intimidated any and all'. And yet 'he becomes almost maternally protective of those who belonged to the circle of his closest students and who readily accepted his leadership'. Today, excerpts from Twardowski's lecture entitled *On the Dignity of the University* are heard cited at various occasions. Among other things, the lecture contains advice for the academic master and teacher, who is 'first and foremost a servant of the objective truth, its representative and its proponent among the young'. I do not use Twardowski's example merely to recall the figure and the words of that veritable master and teacher, but to encourage a little more self-criticism among those who are perhaps too liberal with the term 'scientific school' and erect monuments to the otherwise quite original scholars who – were they alive – would protest at being called masters, or at least some of them would.

The quantity of citations represents a thoroughly novel means of making a particular scholar into an academic master. I am not alone in my misgivings about its credibility and objectivity and have already expressed them more than once. Hence, I will only note that today we may witness how that 'art' has been mastered to perfection, whereby one does not conjure the proverbial 'rabbit out of the hat' but conjures plenty of points out of so few publications. Worse still, original research findings are often hard to come by in those writings. Not to worry, though: these are not the results that really count, but the fact of being published in high-impact journals. Many a former master and teacher in science could learn from these 'masters' of that peculiar 'art', but I suppose that at least some would not be persuaded to engage in such practices, not without difficulty. I have also encountered such masters in my immediate academic environment. I will not mention any of their names, as this may be easily verified using the university's Knowledge Base for an overview of publications by scholars from the AMU Faculty of Philosophy. Let me just add that when it came to evaluating the achievements of such a master in the professorial appointment procedure, the reviewers decided that he did not meet the requirements set out in the current Science and Higher Education Act. Either way, it is much less awkward to talk about the past masters and teachers, or at least those active in a different academic 'backyard' than one's own.

Even so, a few words of supplement may be shared, hoping that they will not be offended – if still alive – or that at least some of their surviving students will not take offence on behalf of those who passed away. Regrettably, I cannot say that I had many such masters while studying history. I had classes with various lecturers, including those who were considered top-notch experts, at least in Poland. However, I have no grounds to say whether they really were, because they did not do anything remarkable enough for me to remember. Meanwhile, the professor who left a strong and positive impression was not only particularly well prepared for the lectures but also stood out due to manners and personal demeanour. In the first several years of my work at the university, I dealt with superiors rather than masters. I could say much about my immediate superior, but some things I would prefer left unsaid. I will only say that he would be surprised (were he still alive) to be told that he was a true master in the field of academic training of philosophers. On the other hand, I must also admit that although he did not help me solve the philosophical problems I faced, he did not make it difficult either. He openly confessed that it was not his métier, adding that I could handle them myself. That faith in my intellectual ability is well worth appreciating, because there were others at the time who thought (despite being unfamiliar themselves with the issues I was trying to tackle) that I was a talentless hack at philosophy and should preferably look for another job. I guess they were sorry when other assessors of my academic achievement did not share that view and supported my applications for a postdoctoral degree and the subsequent professorship.

However, in both early and later periods of my career I never had the luxury of disregarding the opinions of my opponents. Before the 1989 watershed in Poland, those who had the most say in numerous institutes such as mine, were people who at least considered themselves Marxists. Were they conversant with it? It is difficult for me to determine, because I never engaged with Marxism myself. Later though, when the academic 'winds' turned westerly as opposed to blowing from the east, they curiously easily changed 'tack'. However, none of them made an international career and if any of them are still alive, they are unlikely to get there in any case, if only because Marxism practiced in Western countries has invariably been different from the variety practiced in countries that clung to the belief in the infallibility of Karl Marx. Still, I would not like to 'lump' all the purported or real Marxists together. In my immediate environment, there were also philosophers who introduced their own amendments to Marxism. One of them (Leszek Nowak) called it 'non-Marxian historical materialism'. As you may imagine, the orthodox Marxists, of whom there were several at the institute, were not thrilled at the idea. Conceivably, some of them were even pleased that the philosopher was sent for re-education at an internment camp after martial law had been imposed in Poland in 1981.

Schools in science

The first schools appeared in ancient Greek philosophy. They were founded by philosophers who not only had something important to say but were also able to gather around themselves a group of students who developed and popularised their views. Some of them turned out to be as outstanding as their masters and later founded their own schools. This was the case, for example, with the Platonic school, called the Academy of Athens, and with the Peripatetic school founded by one of Plato's students – Aristotle. In the Middle Ages, there was only one school – scholastic (the term *scholastikos* means school), but it has been known for a long time that this term actually covers different trends and tendencies occurring in philosophy and theology of the time. In short: each time had and still has its own type of schools, differing both in the way they were created and how they functioned.

Question marks

First, however, a few fundamental doubts related to the title problem. They appear, among others, in the collective work edited by Janusz Goćkowski and Andrzej Siemianowski, entitled *Schools in Science*. They concern both more general issues (including the sense of the question about the existence of various types of schools in science) and specific ones. For example, Jerzy Szacki prefaces the question of what a scientific school is with the statement that in the 'language of scientific communities this term has all the hallmarks of colloquialism', and throughout the work this term is placed in quotation marks. In turn, Czesław S. Nosal, drawing attention to a number of conditions for the establishment and functioning of schools, claims that in the case of such 'small social groups', the documentary material is always incomplete. The greatest doubts are related to the fact that the documents of interest to the historian of science (...) only to a small extent reflect the climate of small social groups, the informal structure of scientific organisations, etc.' In subsequent studies, the problem of the existence of specific scientific schools in specific sciences is taken up. Those who comment on this topic, of course, organise the image of these schools, but they also highlight a number of question marks related to this issue. Kazimierz Opałek, writing about schools in legal theory, asks: is a neutral research organisation already a school, or is a grouping based on irrational foundations a scientific school, (...) where is the boundary between them and a sect, and also how does a scientific school differ from the so-called directions or trends in science? On the other hand, Elżbieta Pełka-Pelińska and Jadwiga Grabowska, in the summary of their argument on schools in anthropology, propose a controversial division into three types of schools: classical ('focused around the figure of a master'), 'based on the activity of a group connected by non-scientific ideas' and 'based on the proposal of a new pattern of thought (a new paradigm)', adding that these are 'ideal types that can overlap'.

The emergence of various fashions in science is not always harmful. They can significantly contribute to focusing forces and resources (including financial ones) on solving very serious and important social problems. They become harmful only when they begin to live their own lives or even impose on others a way of thinking about scientific correctness and marginalise those who do not want to or cannot obey them. Such fashions in science – as in other areas of life – come and go. However, before they go, they can not only exploit a research problem long after it has already been solved by serious scientists but even add to it such marginal issues that in the battle for obtaining financial resources for research beat the important ones. Even if such a victory adds some seriousness to them, it is not able to make them very serious.

I will not attempt to resolve the questions posed by the authors of this paper. However, I have no doubt that they confirm the thesis that schools in science were and are a diverse and varied phenomenon (with diverse origins, boundaries and methods of functioning). It is of course easier to find your way around what was or is called a scientific school than what meets its more or less contrived model. Of course, this cannot be an excuse for overusing this name. Such a situation occurs, for example, when several scientists who subscribe to a common theory or are only united by a common belief in its explanatory power start talking about a school, and those who are their collaborators or merely support their actions repeat this on various occasions (thus tormenting all those who are indifferent or sceptical about the theory in question). I hope that no one will feel offended by this remark. I will not hide the fact that it is dictated by the actual situation existing in the philosophical community, in which I have been functioning for many years. This concerns the talk about the so-called Poznań methodological school. I have doubts whether such talk is justified. In my opinion, the philosophical school was and is something significant not only in the local backyard, but also beyond its borders.

Glorious examples

I will cite two examples of modern philosophical schools. The first of them appeared at a time when philosophy was just beginning to gain relative independence from theology that honoured tradition and from all the people and institutions that felt obliged to defend this tradition. The beginnings of this independence date back to the seventeenth century. The trial of Galileo showed that even in its first half this independence was fragile, and those who manifested it too boldly encountered serious problems. Galileo, despite being an outstanding mind and the rebellious spirit of his times, did not establish any school. Nor did another great mind of that century, Descartes, formally establish a school. In fact, however, during his lifetime (he died in 1650), people spoke of 'Cartesians' and even banned them from publicly proclaiming their 'audacious' and 'impious' theses (such as that the connection between the soul and the body is 'accidental' and not 'substantial'). Needless to say, this did not prevent Cartesianism from gaining a strong position in the world of philosophy and science; to this day, the so-called *l'esprit cartésien* is associated with such hallmarks of science as rigour, provability, and verifiability of theorems.

If, therefore, we can speak of a Cartesian school (and I see no reason not to), then it was certainly a school of a different type than those founded by ancient sages or medieval theologians. Its leader neither strolled through olive groves philosophising with his students, nor did he shine on university chairs, seducing his listeners with sophisticated Latin. On the contrary, Descartes avoided places like universities (and university professorships) like the plague, and he usually spoke to his actual and potential students by correspondence (this is documented by about 500 of his letters). He responded to the objections of the 'Learned Men' in a similar way (those interested in these responses are referred to his *Meditations on First Philosophy*). There is much to suggest that he was neither the scholar-warrior type (who feels best in direct combat with an opponent), nor the scholar-teacher type (who has a need to teach others), nor even the scholar-mentor type (who absolutely has to instruct someone). Of course, this did not prevent him from becoming a great authority and leader of a philosophical school, as well as a symbol of what is associated with the term 'modern'.

The second honourable example is the Lvov-Warsaw school. Its significance does not come from the fact that it brought radically new ideas or solutions to science – its creators and promoters focused rather on developing ideas that had been known to the scientific community for quite a long time, but in their opinion were not appreciated, or at least applied in scientific practice. These are the same ideas that underlie Cartesianism. The position of this school did not come from the fact that its creator, Kazimierz Twardowski, was a philosopher and scholar of world standing – he was a student of Franz Brentano, a philosopher perhaps not second-rate, but certainly not one whose achievements should be known to anyone with some understanding of philosophy. Instead, it came from the fact that first at the University of Lvov, and later at the University of Warsaw (and several others), a group of philosophers and logicians gathered, many of whom had something important to say, and the creator of this school himself influenced more by his example than by his personal scientific achievements. The result was that more than one of Twardowski's students surpassed their master in achievements and became better known than him outside Poland. Examples include Alfred Tarski (who founded the so-called Californian school of logic in the USA) and philosopher and theologian Józef Maria Bocheński (a long-time lecturer at the University of Fribourg, Switzerland).

Schools in market conditions

It is rather impossible to argue with obvious facts, such as the fact that the scientific community, including the universities most distinguished for science and teaching, have been subjected to the rules of the market economy. This is not yet strongly felt by a large part of our scientists, but for Americans it is such an everyday reality that they have to start with it when planning their plans. The presence of the market there is already noticeable at the level of the fight for students. In order to attract students, the universities there must offer such a product (educational programmes, study conditions) and at such a price that they will not go to the competition from the very beginning (and there are about 4,000 universities in this country). And of course they offer it, competing in the didactic offer and in student care systems (how many people in Poland know what the duties of an advisor or mentor involve?).

The trick is of course to provide good education. In the American context, this means – apart from anything else – education oriented towards the labour market, which turns out to be the main verifier of quality. Similarly with research programmes. They cannot be implemented without genuine scientists. However, this is also not possible without significant financial resources, and these are primarily in the hands of large corporations and secular and religious organisations. They of course spend considerable funds, but above all on research that seems sensible, useful or simply profitable to their decision-makers and advisory bodies. The result is that there is a lot of talk today about the commercialisation of science and academic teaching – not only in the USA, but also in those countries that either already belong to the 'leading economies of the world' or are relatively close behind them.

One may ask whether in discussions on market competitiveness and value (of a scientist, research, diploma) there is still room for schools, masters or even an informal social group that – as in the old schools – would forge ideas, theories and research practices in free discussions? This is not a rhetorical question. Examples of the functioning of authentic scientific figures on the global research and education market show that a lot has changed. Of course, there are still outstanding scientists who are able to combine research with managerial functions. However, these are increasingly rare cases. Increasingly often, however, the latter tasks are performed by not very outstanding scientists or people who do not actually have research qualifications but are well prepared and exceptionally talented in effective action at the interface of science and education on the one hand and the labour market, politics, government and non-governmental organisations on the other. This means that roles and tasks must be divided. However, everyone can benefit from this – including those researchers who, apart from scientific 'tinkering', do little more or are not interested in much more.

Polish realities

Today's Poland is still far from being a market economy – measured by American standards. However, in a situation where there is so much talk about the Lisbon Strategy and the Bologna Process or – which amounts to the same thing – catching up or at least following in America's footsteps, it would not be out of place to say a few words about our academic realities. The market is visible in them, but above all in private higher education. However, what takes place there does not contribute much new to the discussion on the functioning of schools in science. First of all, due to the fact that in the vast majority of them, scientific research plays a secondary role, and the excellence of Polish science does give local prestige (which translates into market value), but it rarely goes beyond their own 'backyard'. The mere expectation of Polish scientists to open up more widely to international cooperation may arouse in them the suspicion that their position is being discredited. It is not necessary for academic staff to obtain a positive periodic assessment. In promotion procedures, such a requirement does appear (especially when applying for the title of professor), but it is formulated so enigmatically that it can be met without completing an internship at some important scientific foreign centre. However you judge it, recognising someone as the founder or member of a scientific school still ennobles, which is especially visible when delivering speeches on the occasion of various *honoris*. However, it is usually a courtesy, and the participants of such ceremonies are well aware that it is not about any school. This does not mean that in Polish realities there are no conditions for the formation and functioning of such academic groups. I am inclined to risk the statement that today they are even better than a dozen or so years ago – just to mention, as an example, the greater opportunities for Polish scientists to participate in international research projects. However, you have to want to and be able to use them.

Celebrities, celebrants and halberdiers

In academic life, roles can be and are variedly scripted and assigned. One possible scenario is to write them out into celebrities, celebrants and halberdiers. However, this requires supplements to clarify the particulars of their functioning, which is what I will attempt to provide here. Let me just say at the outset that they may well reflect the part of it which sometimes applies in science and sometimes happens to live its own life.

The celebrities

This term has Latin roots and for centuries was associated with people holding high ecclesiastical offices (including the papal dignity) and secular positions (including royalty). Today, it denotes those who are relatively widely known chiefly thanks to the media, which for their part do not rely on one's actual achievements but exploit the audience's demand for faces and events that 'sell' well. However, academic life is not a 'secluded island' where the elements of media culture do not penetrate. Moreover, it would not want to be one, as this could mean ending up outside social circulation and even being cut off from the public funds it requires to survive and develop its research and educational potential. The problem begins when it not only opens itself up to such influences but also adopts at least some of the rules that govern media culture. It is quite all right when an academic celebrity promoted in this fashion both enjoys widespread interest and demonstrates achievements that constitute a significant contribution to science or at least encourage serious discussion. I have heard of such celebrities, read about them and even met a few on my academic journey.

The British scientist Stephen W. Hawking deserves to be called a genuine celebrity. However, before he became one, he achieved significant results in theoretical physics (such as the theory of the boundless universe) and showed tremendous talent in popularising his findings (having published several books on the subject, including *A Brief History of Time* and *The Universe in a Nutshell*). He also appeared in television shows and the animated series *Family Guy*. Due to a progressive neurodegenerative disease, he became wheelchair-bound and increasingly dependent on a speech synthesiser to communicate. In the final years of his life, he communicated using an infra-red sensor attached to the frame of his glasses. His struggle to remain in the public eye may have been even more important to many observers than his achievements in theoretical physics. A celebrity of a different kind is – or at least was, until recently – the Slovenian philosopher and cultural scholar Slavoj Žižek. He gained widespread fame and a place on the list of world's 100 greatest 'celebrity philosophers' (inducted there in 2012 by the *Foreign Policy* magazine), not so much thanks to his numerous publications (he is the author of more than fifty books), but through public appearances in which he criticised Western democracy from a left-wing perspective and assertions along the lines of: '"communism" is only the term that signals humanity's step towards a better future'. Žižek did not shy away from using 'strong language' while speaking in public. Although he did not employ such emphatic wording in the speech delivered several years ago at my former department, I saw first-hand how he was able to fill the venue with people who might have been less interested in his views but were definitely drawn by his personality. At that time, representatives of the so-called postmodernism also aroused widespread interest. One of them was the French philosopher Jacques Derrida. His lecture at the University of Silesia in Katowice, held in 1988, witnessed a 'pilgrimage' of avid audience from various academic centres. I did not join those 'pilgrims'. However, I had the opportunity to listen to his opening lecture at the 2002 XXIXe Congrès International de l'ASPLF, organised by the University of Nice. If anyone expected a presentation that went beyond academic standards, they were probably very disappointed. I would even say that it was a classic university lecture. Backstage, Derrida did not behave like an international celebrity, either. On the contrary, he even seemed somewhat overwhelmed by his worldwide fame. Derrida is but one example of a celebrated individual who, simultaneously, is no dedicated celebrant of their own greatness.

The celebrants

In the past, the French King Louis XIV, known as the Sun King, was a great celebrity and celebrant in one. He took court celebrations to a level that other monarchs could hardly surpass (although they tried). However, it must be noted that he also had significant achievements in managing his country. At universities, the role of the chief celebrant statutorily falls to the rector. Those who have attended the inauguration of the academic year or at least watched it online will know how it looks in practice. The ceremony is particularly solemn at the beginning and at the end. The senate and the rectorial body enter the hall to the sound of the university anthem. The rector stands out from the crowd, not only due to his outfit, but also because of their insignia of power, such as the rector's chain and sceptre. The rest of the ceremony varies from university to university, but the major ones always commence with the rector's greeting: *Quod bonum, felix, faustum, fortunatumque sit!* and a triple tap of the sceptre. Even greater variety is seen with the scenarios of university anniversaries. The year 2019 saw the centennial of the University of Poznań, whose celebrations were scheduled over several days and culminated in a procession through the city. The rectorial authorities and the members of senates of all higher schools that later emerged from the University of Poznań walked from the Cathedral Island to the main university auditorium. I took part in it personally (as a member of the senate) and have to admit that it was not only solemn, but also pleasant. The problem with the rectorial celebrations arises when it intrudes on the day-to-day duties of such a university authority. In my academic life, I have not met many such rectors-celebrants, but I can confidently say that the one I came across proved a considerable professional nuisance for me, particularly when I was a vice-dean and had to seek his permission to start a construction project on my campus. Still, this was nothing compared to the hassle the students had with the dean for student affairs, who simply enjoyed chatting with every student who came to him. As a result, there was usually a long queue of inquirers and applicants at his door. The opposite was the case with another vice-dean in charge of student matters, who celebrated his office so much that he would only see students at strictly defined duty hours, and the unfortunates who failed to get in on time wandered around the faculty office seeking help with the head dean or the administrative staff. In any case, I find the former mode of celebrating dean's authority to be superior to the latter.

In academic life, there are also celebrities who merely get their 'five minutes' for grand celebrations. This includes persons who fete anniversaries or farewells upon reaching retirement age. I have attended more than one such event and the scenario is always the same. The celebrant is given a place of honour while successive other celebrants take their turns to vie in eulogies of the esteemed individual. It may pass if what they say is in some way related to their actual accomplishment. Still, on such festive occasions, the goal is not to reiterate well-known facts but, first and foremost, say something that will please the honouree and possibly their closest colleagues. In these 'brutal' times, when hiding insufficiency of one's scientific output is so difficult, it is still possible to 'plaster over' the gaps with teaching and organisational achievements; when these are wanting as well, one can highlight the character traits which made it a delight to work with the honouree or at least recall those moments when the person in question showed extraordinary kindness or courtesy. I cite only a few examples of the laudatory speeches delivered by the celebrants, but their inventiveness goes much further. What reaction does it elicit in those who are only passive participants of such celebrations? In most cases, they respond with a great deal of forbearance; after all, the event is not about presenting the honouree with a tally of shortcomings of which they should be ashamed. It does happen, however, that certain guests (perhaps disgusted by the flattery) leave before the celebrations are over.

The halberdiers

A typical halberd is a two-handed weapon consisting of an axe mounted on a 1.5- to 1.8-metre-long shaft, with a hook on the other end with which a halberdier would pull riders off their horses. Used from the thirteenth century onwards, it was particularly popular with Swiss troops. In 1505, Pope Julius II recruited them to form the Pontifical Guard, so as to be protected against the numerous threats at the time. Although this protection did not always work (as evidenced by the fact that the popes lost control of the huge

Papal States), the Pontifical Guard still exists today and may be seen parading with halberds. Those who accompany the rectors at various university ceremonies, including the inauguration of the academic year, parade with rectorial halberds. They may even have been trained in providing first aid to the rector, but I doubt that the help they are ready to offer is of the 'life and death' variety. Holding the halberd and remaining solemnly serious until the end of the ceremony is what counts. I am joking, of course, though only a little, as I have often witnessed such university ceremonies where the halberdiers were nowhere near making an imposing figure, and what could be read from their faces was in many cases boredom (since they would have already taken part in numerous meetings of the kind) and anticipation for their ordeal to end.

The matter becomes much more serious when the term 'halberdier' is taken more broadly and refers to all those who are supposed to defend university values and greatnesses, but either fail to do so them or defend what has actually little to do with academic values. In communist Poland, such 'halberdiers' at universities would safeguard the only correct ideology. At ecclesiastical universities, they have invariably shielded religious conscience and mindset. In the so-called free Poland, many universities saw numerous changes take place, but the 'halberdiers' ready to fight for the values and greatnesses they consider to be the only right ones are by no means gone. The problem is that in many cases they are barely worth a skirmish. This is particularly difficult to explain to someone who has just been 'ordained' a doctor and is not only celebrating their success with relish but has their family all proud of it as well. I remember that after I had managed to obtain my doctorate in a relatively short time, my supervisor warned me against thinking that I had made it to hog heaven. Meanwhile, I heard from my more experienced colleagues that such a newly 'ordained' doctor is most often a real pain in the neck for their spouse, who has to patiently endure their putting on airs as if they were an expert on everything.

There is a separate group of academic 'halberdiers': individuals who have not produced anything science-wise but had teachers and mentors whom they admired and to whom they owe their long-standing presence at the university. Many a person I have encountered throughout my academic life would defend their greatness, even though the people concerned – had they been alive – would have objected to such a defence. I am not going to mention anyone by name here, but I will say that if anyone still talks about the so-called Poznań school of methodology today, they are mainly people who have a lot to thank its leaders for, as well as their friends or at least persons in the social circle. And yet, I would still rank them higher than the halberdiers who appear on the theatre stage and so very proudly brandish their halberds, although they have no lines to speak. Incidentally, in academic life, that group is highly diverse. It is somewhat saddening to see people parading their professorial titles and bygone academic achievements, while their current activity mainly consists of appearing at occasional ceremonies and chanting praises of those who have not accomplished anything special in science. At the opposite extreme from the 'halberdiers', one will find individuals who neither have such a title nor have been asked to give a speech but made it to the stage mainly because they had mastered the art of surviving and enduring until retirement, sometimes even longer.

Academic climes

Hardly anyone needs convincing that climate plays an important role in human life and coexistence with others. However, the question of what steps should be taken to adapt as best as possible – or at least not to get anything 'nipped by the frost' – may be subject to debate. Naturally, academic climes differ in many respects from the natural atmospheric phenomena.

The cold climates

The views of the philosopher and jurist Charles de Montesquieu concerning the influence of climate on human nature and culture are still of great interest today, and some of his observations appear quite pertinent. He is best remembered for the treaty entitled *The Spirit of the Laws* (with its pioneering ideas which underlie the modern understanding of constitutional law). While one can seriously argue with his general proposition that it was God who laid down the 'immutable laws of nature', it would be rather difficult to challenge the claim that 'man violates them constantly', and that the laws created by people depend not only on those very people but also on their natural environment, including the climate in which they live and interact with others. Thus, he distinguished three essential climatic zones: cold, hot and temperate. The peoples living in the first are characterised not only by resistance to pain, but also by courage and confidence in their strength. Conversely, one of the traits of those living in the hot zone is timidity. In this classification, the peoples inhabiting the temperate zone apparently ranked the best because not only are they able to control their emotions, but also to make the best use of their reason and the riches of the natural habitat. Although according to Montesquieu different nations may be found the latter zone, his description places the French at the fore. This, he asserts, is evident in it being the country of the best scholars, jurists, artists, and philosophers, of course. This may be taken with a pinch of salt, as the author was entitled to local patriotism after all. The only problem is that even today some French people still think and say the same. Still, the 'added value' lies in the division into the three climate zones and the characteristics of certain peoples that Montesquieu formulated. Besides, it is largely true that practically all peoples living in different places and times have been exposed to climate change as well as experienced the pros and cons associated with each zone.

During the so-called Cold War, the academic climes were no different, notably in those countries which participated in the arms race. Even so, the conditions for practicing science were particularly harsh in the Soviet Union. In the times of perestroika, the West learned about the existence of such research centres where the scientific staff were 'barracked' and completely isolated from the outside world. Names such as Tomsk-7 meant little to the average citizen in the Soviet Union, too. It was only after the explosion of a nuclear reactor that the site made it into the newspapers (*Time* considered it one of the largest nuclear disasters). It turned out that location in question was Seversk, a city established in the Tomsk Oblast in 1949, whose current population is just over 100,000. That centre qualifies in the cold zone, not so much because of the low temperatures there (which do not usually exceed –25 degrees Celsius, even in winter), but because the research staff, as well as their family members and supporting personnel were in a sense confined. Obviously, they fared better than the scientists who, in the course of Stalin's purges, ended up in a much colder part of Siberia or facing the NKVD firing squads. In the countries called the 'brotherly nations of the USSR' by the metaphorists and satellite states by the realists, the academic climes varied. In those states whose leaders made it a point of honour to faithfully follow the 'big brother', one did not perhaps create closed cities, but closed research facilities for the ideologically uncertain scholars were indeed established, while those who managed to find employment somewhere else were under surveillance. Although in Poland this did not assume such pathological forms as, for example, in the GDR, many of our scientists were coldly received when 'knocking on the gates of the academia', and even if they were not turned away empty-handed, they would end up either at some provincial university or at the Polish Academy of Sciences (PAN), which has no contact with young students through teaching. On the night of twelfth December into thirteenth December, a great chill swept through Poland, not so much outside one's window, but rather in those circles that had hoped for democratic changes in social life (which included the majority of the academic community). Although the martial law that was formally introduced at the time was lifted on 22 July 1983, it was not until June 1989 that a truly warmer spell set in.

The hot climates

During a hot war – such as World War II – the academic climes were often heated as well, which applied to all countries involved in that conflict. In the Third Reich, research centres were set up where scientists sought to invent the Wunderwaffe (Wonder Weapon) to deal a decisive blow to their opponents. Today, we know that their work on nuclear weapons was quite advanced. This would not have been possible without the contribution of outstanding German physicists, such as Werner Heisenberg (Nobel Prize winner in 1932), who led the team tasked with its construction. After the end of hostilities, the involvement of those scientists in Hitler's expansionist plans became a hot issue. At least some of them 'beat their breasts' and, after being brought to the USA, tried to atone for their sins through commitment to the American nuclear weapons programme, an undertaking which went down in history as the Manhattan Project. It was launched in 1942 and carried out at Columbia University in New York, the University of Chicago and the University of California in Oakland. Atomic bombs were constructed at the Los Alamos National Laboratory in northern New Mexico. Robert Oppenheimer, a physicist and professor at the University of California, became the scientific director of the programme. In the feature film about the latter, Albert Einstein makes a somewhat humorous figure, but the scientist and the atmosphere of heated debate surrounding the research into nuclear bombs was depicted fairly realistically. The enthusiasm of at least some of the co-authors of that success faded after the bombs had been dropped on Japanese cities. It came as a shock to the entire Western world when the USSR carried out the first detonation of an atomic bomb at the Semipalatinsk nuclear test site in August 1949. An investigation ensued, searching for those who had supplied the American documentation to the Soviets. Oppenheimer was among the suspects. Although he was acquitted by the court in 1954, the American authorities stripped him of leadership in the project and rescinded his access to classified files. The hunt for communists and their sympathisers in the USA went well beyond the academic community, spanning the government, the military and the journalists. Known afterwards as 'McCarthyism' (after Senator J. R. McCarthy, the head of the Senate Permanent Subcommittee on Investigations), it bred an atmosphere of fear and suspicion, as the 'Communist infiltration' was tracked down by any means available.

In the countries of the Eastern Bloc, efforts to ferret out the 'enemies of the people' were undertaken practically from the moment the Communists seized power in those countries. The authors of *The Black Book of Communism* add in the subtitle that it is a history written with *crimes, terror and repression*, were communists persecuted other communists. Stalin gave a particularly 'hot' welcome to the delegates at the seventeenth Congress of the All-Union Communist Party (Bolsheviks) in 1934, as 1,108 of the 1,996 participants were arrested and executed on his orders. 'All scholarly fields with the slightest connection to politics, ideology, economics, or defence were also affected. The main figures in the aeronautics industry, notably Andrei Tupolev (the renowned aeronautical engineer) and Sergei Korolev (one of the founders of the first Soviet space programme), were arrested and sent to NKVD research centres [...]'. In the 'brotherly' (satellite) countries of the USSR, a number of communists strove at least to stir up suspicion and distrust as they could not do exactly likewise, while others approached such measures with more distance. It was no different in the People's Republic of Poland. Its history was to some extent written by leaders such as B. Bierut, who zealously carried out Moscow's orders, as well as W. Gomułka and E. Gierek, who were reluctant to do so and delayed their implementation. The 'hot' spring of 1968, initiated by the students at Warsaw universities, was an incidental event, but it was a clear signal that their rule was coming to an end.

The moderate climates

These may be the most difficult to identify because what may be considered a sign of moderation in some nations may be seen at least as a token of indifference – if not a kind of extremity – in others. Naturally, one could follow Montesquieu's advice and assume that the Romance nations have a natural proclivity for moderation. In my academic life, I have often dealt with the French, Italians and the Spanish. As for the latter, I had the opportunity to find out the meaning of the Spanish expression '*mañana*'. A dictionary will tell you that it can mean 'morning' and 'in the future', as well as 'tomorrow will be better' (to live or to do something). In practice, however, it means that one should not be in too much of a hurry with anything, and that whatever might be done today, can just as well – or even better – be done tomorrow or later. Its Polish equivalent is the colloquial 'podchorąży zawsze zdąży [lit. the ensign will always make it]'; he might gain an officer's star or two, but if they procrastinate, they are unlikely to make it to general or the title of professor at a university. Based on occasional contacts with Italians, I am inclined to venture that hardly any of them apply this principle in practice: they are more inclined to do something 'for yesterday' than for tomorrow and appear surprised on being told that it is already too late for something. A French person is more likely to look for a 'golden mean' and, if they do not find it, they will resort to a barrage of polite words to 'sweeten' their tardiness. There is a widespread belief that the typical Englishman is a phlegmatic individual who will think long and hard before taking any action, deliberating whether it is worth their while. There is something to it. At least, this is confirmed to some extent by the description of the atmosphere at All Souls College, Oxford University, where Prof Andrzej Walicki stayed in 1966–67 and in 1973. In his eyes, 'it was a completely different, charmingly anachronistic world. Meals taken together in the evening, dressed in gowns, attended by servants, with the established rituals strictly observed (…). the entire atmosphere is thoroughly pervaded by the ideal of the gentleman, that is, a man who does not hurry, who has time for everything, and who is confident of his own worth …' This college can afford it, being one of the wealthiest at the university (its assets exceed £144 million), while its faculty are not involved in student education.

In our academic realities, it is the Polish Academy of Sciences who are exempt from the obligation to teach students. The problem is that its institutes are not rich enough to afford communal meals for their employees (let alone servants); in fact, they can barely ensure their professors a decent pay. I remember how, during the fervent debates concerning the draft of the Act 2.0, one of them asked the then head of the ministry, Jarosław Gowin: 'Minister, do you want to starve us?' Today, the salaries of most academic staff have improved, but not sufficiently to enable them to focus solely on research. Obviously, you could say: 'as the work, so the pay'. However, such a mindset and claim are mainly reserved for those who have excessive financial aspirations but subscribe to 'mañana' as far as work is concerned. If, on top of that, they live in an environment which tolerates their moderate commitment to professional duties, it is almost certain that the gap between their aspirations and the outcomes of their research will deepen. However, a number of scholars in the academic community pay little attention to salaries but nevertheless improve their qualifications and carry out their duties with considerable dedication. Do they constitute a vast majority? This is rather a rhetorical question. If that were the case, Polish universities and research institutions would probably stand much higher in the prestigious rankings of the world's leading academic centres. Still, you have to start somewhere. Leaving the surrender of financial aspirations aside, my suggestion is that one should start by honestly assessing academic qualifications and matching them to the existing possibilities of engaging in research. Needless to say, these qualifications can and should be constantly improved. Today's open borders and the opportunities to learn from those who are better than us make it genuinely easier. However, it is not only necessary to want to travel, but also not to treat such trips as mere tourist excursions.

Politicisation of universities

I believe that universities fared best when they were able to maintain considerable distance from politicians and politics. However, this has not always been possible. Hence the question: how much politics can or should there be in the life of higher schools, and what kinds of politics may be beneficial or, conversely, do more harm than good? Regrettably, no definite answer can be offered here, but a few examples are well worth considering.

Historical cases

I prefer to use the term 'case' because it connotes a characteristic event better than the notions of occurrence or situation. At any rate, I would not want these examples of the close ties between politics and universities to be treated either as historical titbits or as 'accidents at work' that might be used today as a 'boogeyman' to scare people. Naturally, no case should be used as conclusive precedent, but it may at least prompt more profound reflection on the issue, if not contribute to its solution. So much for the nomenclature. A brief explanation is also due regarding the personification of these cases. I treat this as a mental shortcut rather than an expression of the belief that the entire problem of politics and politicians being involved in the life of universities can be reduced to the actions of one or more persons.

The first such figure is Henry VIII, king of England. During his reign (1509–1547), there were only two universities in the country – Cambridge and Oxford – both of which were in fact religious institutions, just as other European universities at the time. Consequently, they were supervised by ecclesiastical hierarchs: the Pope and the English Catholic bishops in the early period of the reign and, after Henry VIII and the English Parliament had 'divorced' Rome in 1534–1536, that authority was assumed by the king and the hierarchs of the Church of England, commonly referred to as the Anglican Church. Importantly, the ruler supported the needs and aspirations of the English universities, while university professors repaid the favour by backing the aspirations of Henry VIII. How that worked in practice is described, for example, by George Macaulay Trevelyan in *English Social History*. The author states that even under Henry VII, bishops 'were first and foremost royal nominees and civil servants', while higher schools showed great preference for those intellectual currents that later brought forth such religious reformers as Luther and Calvin. However, Henry VIII was neither an adherent nor even a sympathiser of their teachings. On the contrary, he fought against them so zealously that Pope Clement VII awarded him the title of 'defender of the faith' in recognition of his merit in the field. It is also worth recalling that the two English universities witnessed their heyday during the reign of Henry VIII's daughter, Elizabeth I. Among the many contributing factors, one should mention the policies of the queen, who understood both the educational needs of her country and the proclivity of the faculty to lead lazy lives. In the long-term, however, the reliance on the political 'protective umbrella' brought about the downfall of those universities in the eighteenth century.

Hitler's case shares something in common with that of Henry VIII and the continuators of his university-related policies, namely that it involved a country with centuries-long academic traditions. After all, quite a few German universities may be credited with significant contributions to European culture, including the University of Heidelberg, founded in 1386 by Elector Palatine Ruprecht, and the University of Leipzig, founded by the Saxon dukes Friedrich I the Belligerent and Wilhelm II the Rich. Many significant figures in Polish culture studied at the latter university as late as the first half of the sixteenth century. The 1933 rise to power of politicians such as Hitler meant that those universities were forced back into the darkest of times. First, the incumbent rectors were dismissed and new ones appointed (with the title of 'University Führer'), while the senates and faculty councils became 'National Socialist boards of trustees'. This was directly followed by the policy of so-called 'uniformisation' and 'Aryanization' (whereby the academic community was divided into 'Aryans', 'half-Aryans' and 'non-Aryans'), implemented by the Third Reich authorities and the newly established Reich Ministry of Science, Education and Culture. As a result, Jewish scholars were expelled from German universities, while theories formulated by non-Aryans – such as Albert Einstein's theory of relativity – were removed from curricula.

The same may be said of Stalin, though one of the differences between him and the previous case is that he was born and grew up in a country with relatively few universities. The higher schools which did function there did not stand out in terms of quality of education and research. The two largest Russian universities, St Petersburg (founded in 1724 by tsar Peter the Great) and Moscow (founded in 1755 by empress Elizabeth Petrovna) were modelled on German universities, but even the greatest commitment of Russia's intellectual elites at the time could not make up for the lack of staff that quality education and research requires. Stalin's policies entailed a wave of repressions that swept across the academic community to drive out the 'enemies of the people'. Almost all fields of knowledge (including natural and mathematical sciences) and education were subordinated to the communist ideology and the authority of commissars. The authors of *The Black Book of Communism* cite exact figures showing how many people suffered from the repressions. In late 1944, the commissars 'knocked' on the doors of Polish universities in the east, such as the Jan Kazimierz University in Lvov and the Stefan Batory University in Vilnius, and 'sent packing' those professors whom they considered to be 'class enemies' or politically unreliable.

'Velvet revolutions'

The heading refers to the 1989 events in Czechoslovakia, which led to the collapse of the regime known as 'people's democracy' and enfranchised those whose voice constitutes the strength of parliamentary democracies, that is, ordinary citizens. However, it may also denote the many transformations in Western countries that brought about profound changes in various spheres of social life, including the academia. The 1968 events in France in 1968 are an example of such a revolution; in its wake, higher education in that country saw a fundamental shift. There is no need to go into the details here, as the matter has been very extensively studied and discussed. Instead, I would like to make a few observations about the changes that are referred to as the Bologna Process. The latter involved the signing of the *Bologna Declaration* on 19 June 1999 by the ministers in charge of education and science in EU member states. The signatory commitments stipulated in that relatively short document meant truly revolutionary changes in the organisation of public higher educations across the EU; among other things, the universities were to depart from one-stage master's programmes and transition to a 'system essentially based on two main cycles, undergraduate and graduate', as well as adopt a point-based system to account for the years and stages of university studies (known as ECTS). In the wake of later conferences of the ministers and the declarations they signed, one not only began to speak of the European Higher Education Area but also approach that framework as an integrating and, after some time, already largely integrated system of higher education. Is this a policy, the derivative of politics? It is, without a doubt. Would it mean that it is making broad inroads into many European universities? There can be little doubt about that either. The same applies to research. Although it operates under a different name than education policy (such as 'EU framework programmes') and manner of its implementation differs from the latter (by e.g. setting priorities and specific research tasks), its premises invoke essentially the same notions, that is, 'cohesion', 'innovation', 'efficiency', and speak of opportunities that those who do not join such undertakings can only dream of.

One might ask if there is anything wrong with pursuing such a policy and encouraging those qualified to provide academic instruction and conduct high-quality scientific research to participate. A possible answer may be found in Krystian Szadkowski's book entitled *Uniwersytety jako dobro wspólne* [*Universities as a Common Good*]. At the outset, the author cites the example of Clark Kerr, former president of the University of California, who 'treated the university like another production sector, this time one that fed the dynamically developing knowledge industry', and whose policy contributed to 'a wide stream of money' flowing into the university. In consequence, it became the 'flagship' (with the 'bureaucrat captain' C. Kerry on its 'bridge') of American higher education. However, the price that had to be paid was 'forced industrialisation' of the university and 'melting into the surrounding social fabric'. The author also highlights other corollaries of that policy, namely 'hybridisation' of higher schools, that is, 'the blending of the orders of what is private and public', as well as the 'hegemony-drive' of the American model of higher education, in which the universities capable of attracting the most funding – and thus offer the best working conditions and salaries to the academics – come out on top. One could say that this is America's problem. If that were the case, neither Szadkowski nor others who study the changes in education today would draw attention to the dangers of uncritically adopting American solutions in Europe. This, of course, applies to copying the American higher education system, and to thinking and talking about universities as a kind of 'business', 'enterprise' or 'company' in which positive balance of income and expenditure is what counts above all else – because otherwise it will be declared bankrupt or forced to adopt a recovery programme that usually involves 'downsizing' its workforce. Perhaps this is plain as pikestaff, but one of the reasons why I raise the issue is that terms such as 'commercialisation of research' are used all too readily in present-day debate concerning the problems of higher education. They are either downright borrowed from business language or, at least, blur the differences and boundaries between the economy and scientific research.

The latter issue is directly related to the politicisation of universities, not only from the top down (by politicians with decision-making power in various central bodies), but also from the bottom up, that is, by university staff in the senates, faculty councils, trade and self-governance unions, etc., as well as by persons who are not members of such bodies but speak out publicly and take sides in the ongoing disputes and political conflicts. Such politicisation of universities is undoubtedly one of the most sensitive areas of academic life. This is partly due to the fact that in a civil society (for which the battles in the 'velvet' revolutions are fought) each of its member has the right, and often the duty, to take the public floor on issues that they consider to be socially relevant. However, the line between them being a 'John Smith' (regardless of whether they have an academic title or not) and becoming a representative of a particular university is fluid and relatively easy to cross, notably in those media which seek to lend credibility to the statements of such a person by underscoring their academic affiliation (and hardly any outlet would pass the opportunity). What is more, such individuals rarely object to being thus presented in the media, not even so much because they desire some eminence, but because they are deeply convinced of championing a just cause or being on the right side of a political controversy, whereby they can serve that cause and their university as well.

If anyone finds that the above examples of academic life becoming aligned with politics are some kind of historical 'twaddle', they should take a closer look at what happened quite recently during the tenure of Przemysław Czarnek as Minister of Science and Education. I would be inclined to say that his administration will mark a black page – rather than a mere 'red card' – in the history of Polish universities. Is this a political statement? Unquestionably so.

Enthusiasm in science

One can get by without major enthusiasm, but it is difficult to achieve anything meaningful in life, including academic life. That being said, it must be applied in such doses so as not to impair our ability to overcome the circumstances that stand in the way to achieving our goals. It is good to combine it with experience, but the latter can be both encouraging as well as discourage one from action. Either way, it may be worthwhile to see what it was like for those who accomplished much in science.

A handful of examples

Let us start with René Descartes. Renowned as a philosopher, he also contributed significantly to mathematics. It may be recalled that he formulated the basics of analytical geometry (one of the branches of mathematics today) and helped liberate physics from the Aristotelian assumptions that over time became a kind of 'stumbling block' for the discipline. However, he would have achieved little if he had not received a solid education at the Jesuit college in La Flèche (which he attended from the age of 8 to 16). Although he would later present his teachers in less than a positive light, he admitted in his *Discourse on the Method* that he owed his 'predilection for mathematics' to them. That fondness directly translated into the philosophical and scientific enthusiasm that accompanied his entire scholarly journey. All the solutions he advanced had their source and justification in approaching mathematics as if it were one great book which contains the wisdom of the entire world. One only needs to be able to read it, being aided by adequate mathematical competence.

Naturally, Descartes was convinced that he possessed it and, until the end of his relatively short life (he died at 54), he attempted to present the principles governing a world in which everything tallied mathematically. However, philosophers such as Gottfried W. Leibniz and scientists such as I. Newton were seriously doubtful on that score. They considered themselves more mathematically qualified than their predecessors to reconstruct the mathematical order of the world that would be outlined in their treaties. However, not a single such reconstruction published to date has gone undisputed.

Charles Darwin did not lack enthusiasm for research, either. The British scientist did not engage with mathematics but achieved his greatest success in the field now known as evolutionary biology. His magnum opus was *On the Origin of Species*, published in 1859. It may be noted that Darwin had a broader academic background, having first studied medicine at the University of Edinburgh, from which he transitioned later to natural sciences at the University of Cambridge. Even so, this would have been of little use if he had not been passionate about biological research from an early age. That enthusiasm prompted him to take part in natural history expedition aboard *HMS Beagle* (which lasted from December 1831 to October 1836). His biographers, M. White and J. Gribbin, state that he became friends with the ship's captain, Richard FitzRoy, who 'spent hours discussing biology and geology with Darwin'. According to the above authors, some of the phenomena observed by Darwin during the expedition caused his apprehension (e.g. the behaviour of the natives who greeted them 'talking and making gestures with great rapidity'), others provoked objection (e.g. the conduct of the land-owning 'Spaniards who treated the locals even more appallingly than the British did further north'), and still other things aroused his enthusiasm (e.g. he was 'enthusiastic about the role of the missionary'). All that was important, but not crucial in making the discovery that won him an eminent place in the history of science. His biographers agree, citing such foundations of that success as Darwin's study of 'the wildlife of the Brazilian jungle [where he] was particularly fascinated with the beetles and other insects living on the jungle floor'. This fascination stayed with him for the rest of his life, as he would think and speak with delight about the research on his 'beloved barnacles' ('extremely small creatures (each one only the size of a pin's head)') and 'return enthusiastically to the kind of work on which he had first cut his teeth as a naturalist'.

The German sociologist, lawyer and economist Max Weber showed tremendous enthusiasm for scientific research as well. Although Weber did not live to see old age (1864–1920), he achieved enough during his relatively short life to be recognised as one of the foremost representatives of social sciences and humanities. His seminal *Economy and Society: An Outline of Interpretive Sociology* is in fact the kind of 'outline' that take over a thousand pages to describe the multiple principles governing the enormously diverse social world. I will not quote excerpts from that work here but instead draw on the lecture that Weber gave at the University of Munich in 1917. Entitled *Science as a Vocation* (*Wissenchaft als Beruf*), it paints a picture of a scholar who has 'the capacity to put on blinders, so to speak, and to come up to the idea that the fate of his soul depends upon whether or not he makes the correct conjecture at this passage of this manuscript'. The scholar who lacks such skills 'will never have what one may call the "personal experience" of science. Without this strange intoxication, ridiculed by every outsider; without this passion, this "thousands of years must pass before you enter into life and thousands more wait in silence" – according to whether or not you succeed in making this conjecture; without this, you have no calling for science and you should do something else. For nothing is worthy of man as man [of science] unless he can pursue it with passionate devotion'. There may be a hint of humour there, but Weber was far from joking, whether in his academic life or in his portrayal of the lives of all those who set themselves ambitious goals and persevere to achieve them. This is corroborated by another major achievement of his, *The Economic Ethics of the World Religions*, spanning Taoism, Confucianism, Hinduism, Buddhism and Judaism.

A few general remarks

Based on the above examples of scholars who manifested their enthusiasm for science in various ways, one can venture several, more general observations. The first – perhaps the most general of all – boils down to the statement that the enthusiasm of scholars is constantly under pressure from those who expect them to produce tangible results, and if they also spend a lot of money on their research, the pressure can be so great that the scholars can no longer live on enthusiasm alone and have to take measures that would enable them to satisfactorily account for those funds. Those who carried out self-funded research or used the means of their immediate family (such as Descartes and Darwin) are in the most comfortable situation. However, being a full-time university professor means that one either lives at the taxpayer's expense (in countries where higher education is publicly funded) or at the expense of those who pay for it out of their own pockets. This may either boost the enthusiasm of scientists or 'quench' it, so much so that 'fire' merely smoulders and, as is feared, may go out at any moment. Today, the pressure to achieve the most substantial and fastest results in science is so great that even those who still invoke the enthusiasm of scientists do not consider it a major driving force behind scientific work. Money is the primary concern, at any rate. Although Weber disputed that in the aforementioned lecture and his sentiment is shared by quite a few contemporary scholars, there is little they can do when terms such as 'human capital' or 'enterprise' (denoting the university where they are employed) have entered academic vocabulary. Obviously, one can call upon scholars not to lose their 'spirit' of enthusiasm. Still, there is no argument that they will remain deaf to such appeals when they are required to heed the 'we pay and we demand' on a daily basis, while if they fail to comply, out the door (of universities or other research institutions) they go.

The situation is quite dramatic particularly in those countries that are already rich and would like to grow even richer in the future. This includes the United States and many Western European countries. So far, Poland is not one of them, but does it mean that its scientists can afford the enthusiasm that does not translate into hard currency? Not necessarily. A number of the reforms implemented in the so-called free Poland sought to effect such a conversion, including the reforms of science and higher education. Since the early 1990s, we have constantly heard that Polish economy is not efficient enough, and that Polish universities and research institutes may cost less than their counterparts in Western countries, but they also 'produce' an inferior 'range' of students and scientific solutions. Academics who have spoken on the matter have often opposed and continue to oppose such notions, while if they happen to agree, they immediately name the source of their shortcomings: the underfunding of their research. For the time being, however, no one can predict when much more substantial funds will be allocated to scientific research and development in the national budget.

The waiting for the 'big money' or the idea entertained by politicians that world-class results in science can be accomplished without it are not the only threats to the enthusiasm of scholars. Many mundane circumstances of life can dampen it too, as some do not have to worry about surviving until the next pay day, whereas others have to count every penny. The former group included both Descartes and Darwin. Weber, on the other hand, may not have lived in poverty, but he owed it to the salary earned by professors at German universities. However, none of them practiced the so-called applied sciences, which have always been the most capital-intensive. Does this mean that there is still room for enthusiasm in theoretical inquiry and, possibly, in social sciences and the humanities? That would be a risky proposition to say the least. One could readily cite examples which demonstrate that enthusiasm is relatively easy to 'extinguish' with unfair reviews in promotion procedures or excessive demands from university superiors. I have often been assessed by other scholars and appointed to review the achievements of applicants for academic promotion. I have also had the opportunity to find out about the practices of other reviewers. Within that particular community, some take care not to cause any harm – heaven forbid – to the people they evaluate, but some would rather have the latter 'steamrolled' over. Maybe I exaggerated a little there, so let me just add that I have encountered opinion-givers who would enthusiastically scour the assessed output to find various kinds of shortcomings. Simultaneously, they did not want to or were unable to see the positives that would be evident even to the visually impaired. Perhaps I have exaggerated again (but only a little). After all, I am just one of many who could offer examples of the kind.

My enthusiasm

Each of the general remarks above is based on some of my personal academic experiences, better and worse alike. I must admit that I embarked on that life with plenty of enthusiasm and faith that I could achieve significant results in academic work and that others would at least not hinder me, even if they chose not to help. That turned out something of a miscalculation on my part, because some people I came across during my academic career believed – for reasons known only to themselves – that I should look for another job. At one critical point, I was seriously on the verge of being dismissed from the position of assistant professor, which would require me to look for employment elsewhere. Although it did not come to that, it delayed my obtaining the postdoctoral degree by a few years. There is a saying that 'what does not kill you, makes you stronger'. Indeed, it made me strong enough that I subsequently became a full professor in a relatively short time. It did not kill my enthusiasm for engaging with the philosophy that had been my chief research interest from the outset (French thought), but it stripped me of my somewhat naive belief that holding a professorship alone means decency, and that when such a professor speaks – even if not all too wisely – they know what they are talking about.

Speculativism in science

The saying that science came into being 'in labour pains' is off the mark, insofar as such pains happen once in a while and last a relatively short time. Even so, the birth of science took centuries, and there is no guarantee that what is associated with the term today is a 'child' immune enough to speculativism to survive into adulthood. In any case, it is not such a picture of health that it cannot be thus harmed.

Pythagorean speculativism

Most likely, many people see mathematics as a realm of rigour and provability whose outcomes cannot questioned by anyone who properly applies its rules. One of these rules is the Pythagorean theorem, used to calculate the length of the third side of a right-angled triangle when the lengths of the other two sides are known. It is attributed to Pythagoras of Samos. The problem is not that it had already been known, but that the scientist admired by many generations did not write anything himself and all information about his achievements is second-hand. Much depends on which of those accounts we will draw. Some present him as a demigod, while others speak of a scientist who was able to go beyond mathematics and explore specific phenomena such as earthquakes. An attempt to combine both narratives is made in the *Lives of Pythagoras* by Porphyry, written at the turn of the 4th century AD. In their light, Pythagoras was not only able to accurately predict an earthquake, but also 'chased a pestilence, suppressed violent winds and hail, calmed storms both on rivers and on seas, for the comfort and safe passage of his friends', and 'while his thoughts were on this work intent, all things existent, easily he viewed, through ten or twenty ages making search. (...) He referred his origin to those of past ages (...) [and] showed to his disciples that the soul is immortal'. According to Iamblichus' *Pythagoric Life*, written at the same time, the scholar 'gave completion to the science of the celestial orbs, and unfolded the whole of it by arithmetical and geometrical demonstrations'. His students, the Pythagoreans 'honoured music, medicine and divination' and believed numbers to possess different powers. Having found ten to be a perfect number, they presumed that there were ten planets in the solar system, moving in a circular orbit: the most perfect form of motion.

In the late sixteenth and the early seventeenth century, Johannes Kepler demonstrated that the planets orbit following an elliptical path. However, he propounded a kind of mathematicism in astronomy whereby harmony existed in the space between the planets, informed by the concept of 'friendly polygons and tessellations of planes' as well as panpsychism, according to which 'an animistic interpretation of earthly and psychic bodies creates the possibility of a connection between the physical, organic and mental realms'. According to B. Tuchańska, 'in Kepler's world, everything is connected, "the geometry of the planets influences the human soul," while the proportions of planetary harmony correspond to the proportions of harmony in music. Without a doubt, there was no greater visionary among the astrologers'. However, Kepler had a few successful competitors, such as the Swiss physician, alchemist and astrologer Paracelsus. In the opinion of the latter, 'man is a child of the Microcosm and carries all the mineral elements within'. The world, on the other hand, is 'permeated' with the fluids that may be used to treat the sick. Ultimately, Paracelsus is considered a pioneer of modern toxicology.

Newtonian speculativism

In his fundamental work, *Mathematical Principles of Natural Philosophy*, Isaac Newton tackles more than one of the earlier speculations concerning the natural world, including the so-called vortex theory which, aiming to answer the question of why 'matter revolves around its centre', enjoyed considerable recognition. In Book II of his treatise, Newton he states that 'the hypothesis of vortices is utterly irreconcilable with astronomical phaenomena, and rather serves to perplex than explain the heavenly motions'. In Book III, however – *On the System of the World* – he begins by formulating its four rules, the third of which asserts 'by experiments and astronomical observations, that all bodies about the Earth, gravitate towards the Earth; and that in proportion to the quantity of matter which they severally contain (…) Their gravity is diminished as they recede from the Earth'. He then presents the findings of Borelli, Townley and Cassini, which suggest that 'the forces by which the circumjovial planets are continually drawn off from rectilinear motions, and retained in their proper orbits, tend to Jupiter's centre; and are reciprocally as the squares of the distances of the places of those planets from that centre. (…) The same thing we are to understand of the planets which encompass Saturn (…) and of Mercury and Venus, and the other circumsolar planets (…) There is, therefore, a power of gravity tending to all the planets…' Hence the conclusion that 'the force of gravity which tends to any one planet is reciprocally as the square of the distance of places from that planet's centre'. In addition, there are numerous graphs and computations which prove that all this involves 'mathematical principles' and none other. It would be difficult to find anything speculative about it. The encouragement to speculate only appears in the *General Scholium* at the end of the work. It states that 'this most beautiful system of the sun, planets, and comets, could only proceed from the counsel and dominion of an intelligent and powerful Being. (…) This Being governs all things, not as the soul of the world, but as Lord over all; and on account of his dominion, he is wont to be called Lord God, pantokrator, or Universal Ruler. (…) The Supreme God is a Being eternal, infinite, absolutely perfect; but a being, however perfect, without dominion, cannot be said to be Lord God'. And that is that.

The problem is that that Being is not subject to the same mathematical principles as the natural world. Now, whether it is subject to the principles that theologians follow when delineating images of the Christian God may speculated on, which many have done. Citing Newton's notes discovered in 1936, his biographer Frank E. Manuel claims that in the later decades the scholar devoted all his free time to analysing Christian prophecies and that 'viewed in the light of the religious dedication of all his works, Newton's secret researches were a form of daily prayer and communion with God'. Still, even in-depth studies cannot answer whether it was the God whose existence his closest academic milieu believed. Let us recall that he was a professor at Trinity College, Cambridge, but even with the best will in the world, it cannot be demonstrated that theological speculations led Newton to acknowledge the existence and agency of such a Trinity.

Speculativism among contemporary physicists

The realm of these speculations is diverse and varied enough to yield material for more than one extensive monograph. Here, I will confine myself to mentioning those physicists who gained eminence in the discipline and whose speculations have sparked invigorating debate in the long-standing deliberations about the Universe. Albert Einstein, whose foremost achievements include the special and general theory of relativity, was undoubtedly one such scientist, In 1917, he came forward with an addition: the theory of the universe, which he chose to call 'geometry of the Universe'. In contrast to both Euclidean and Riemannian geometry, it constitutes a 'physical interpretation of geometry' in which 'the universe is spatially finite. This must be so, if there is a mean density of the ponderable matter in universal space differing from zero. The smaller that mean density, the greater is the volume of universal space. (…) it seems impossible to estimate the mean density'. 'Assuming that we know, let us say, the statistical distribution of the stars in the Milky Way, as well as their masses, then by Newton's law we can calculate the gravitational field and the mean velocities which the stars must have, so that the Milky Way should not collapse under the mutual attraction of its stars, but should maintain its actual extent. Now if the actual velocities of the stars, which can, of course, be measured, were smaller than the calculated velocities, we should have a proof that the actual attractions at great distances are smaller than by Newton's law. From such a deviation it could be proved indirectly that the universe is finite. It would even be possible to estimate its spatial magnitude'. In this vision, the universe not only appears as finite, but also spherical (with a three-dimensional generalisation of the surface of a sphere), and having its own 'radius' (determined by its total mass). Was it a thoroughly scientific theory? Not necessarily. Its scientific validity would be questioned in 1922 by the Russian physicist and mathematician Alexander Friedmann and in 1924 by the American astronomer Edwin Hubble.

The above scientists are mentioned by Stephen Hawking in his *Brief History of Time*. He notes that 'Friedmann made two very simple assumptions about the universe: that the universe looks identical in whichever direction we look, and that this would also be true if we were observing the universe from anywhere else. From these two ideas alone, Friedmann showed that we should not expect the universe to be static'. In 1924, Hubble demonstrated that 'our galaxy is only one of some hundred thousand million that can be seen using modern telescopes, each galaxy itself containing some hundred thousand million stars. (…) Stars are so far away that they appear to us to be just pinpoints of light. We cannot see their size or shape. So how can we tell different types of stars-apart? For the vast majority of stars, there is only one characteristic feature that we can observe – the colour of their light. Newton discovered that if light from the sun passes through a triangular-shaped piece of glass, called a prism, it breaks up into its component colours (its spectrum) as in a rainbow. By focusing a telescope on an individual star or galaxy, one can similarly observe the spectrum of the light from that star or galaxy. (…) Moreover, we find that certain very specific colours are missing from stars' spectra, and these missing colours may vary from star to star'. In 1927, Georges Lemaître – Belgian theologian and astronomer (professor at the University of Louvain) – published an article entitled *A Homogeneous Universe of Constant Mass and Increasing Radius*, accounting for the radial velocity of extragalactic nebulae, in which he formulated the thesis that the initial state of the universe was a state of high density, which he called the 'primeval atom'. Its big bang apparently triggered the expansion of the universe. Hubble integrated this explanation of the onset of the universe into his theory. In modern cosmology, it is known as Hubble's law.

Research into the expansion of the universe in later years led to the conclusion that 'our galaxy – like others – must contain a large amount of "dark matter," which cannot be seen directly, but which we know is definitely there because we observe its gravitational effect on the orbits of stars in galaxies. Moreover, since most galaxies belong to clusters, we can deduce the presence of even more dark matter between galaxies by studying its effect on the movement of galaxies. When dark matter is added to the mass of the stars, we still only have one tenth of the density needed to stop the expansion. However, we cannot exclude the existence of another type of matter distributed almost evenly throughout the universe, which could increase the average density of matter to the critical value needed to stop the expansion. In summary, according to the observational data we currently have, the universe will probably expand, but we can only be sure that if the universe is ever to collapse, it will not happen for another 10 billion years, because it has been expanding for at least that long. This shouldn't worry us too much: by that time – if we don't colonise areas outside the Solar System – humanity will no longer exist, as it will die out with the Sun'. An important addition to this vision of the universe is the discovery of many such stars whose 'radiant light from their surfaces cannot be seen because it has been drawn back by gravity, but we can detect their presence through their gravitational pull. Today, we call such objects black holes...' However, according to Hawking, they are not as black as previously thought.

Quasi-scientific assumptions and beliefs

Since ancient times, Western culture has seen a fair share of assumptions and the associated beliefs that purported to be scientific knowledge. However, they were not and could not be considered as such until they satisfied the requirements of that knowledge. Over time, some have been determined to be false and ousted from the realm of science. On the other hand, a proportion would ultimately meet those requirements, becoming part of scientific knowledge. Still, both are worth taking a closer look at, since even those that proved invalid contributed to advancements in science.

The traditions of antiquity

Next to Pythagoras of Samos, Thales of Miletus also wrote an important chapter in the history of mathematics. His theorems on the inscribed triangle and the divisibility of a circle by its diameter are still taught to schoolchildren today. However, Thales' interests and accomplishments went far beyond mathematics as he engaged with astronomy (predicting the solar eclipse of 28 May 585 BC) and physics in the broadest sense. As for the latter, he was less interested in the individual manifestations of the material world than in the general principles (which the Greeks called *arche*) operating at the beginning of the world's existence. He also studied the properties of the 'magnetic stone and amber' and assumed that they possessed a spiritual element. Incidentally, he was not alone in this belief. Numerous ancient philosophers and scholars subscribed to the notion that everything that really exists has its soul. Later on, fewer and fewer scholars would be willing to espouse such broadly understood hylozoism, but as late as the twentieth century there were some (such as Louis Pasteur), who – under the banner of so-called vitalism – identified it in various living organisms. Today, the proponents of a revised version of vitalism are known as emergentists. They may be found not only in biology and psychology, but also in ethology and primatology. A prominent example in the latter field is the British scientist Jane Goodall, who studies the social learning processes and modes of action in chimpanzees.

Epicureanism may also prompt some serious consideration of the viability of quasi-scientific assumptions and beliefs in culture. Today, the views of Epicurus of Samos seem to be a topic of interest mainly to philosophers but, for many centuries, they posed a challenge for Christian theologians and the representatives of various natural sciences as well. Epicurean ethics was particularly prone to cause substantial controversy. Both its supporters and opponents perceived it as thoroughly naturalistic and, to some extent, they still do. However, while the former did not find anything wrong with it, the latter – on the contrary – often asserted it to be morally reprehensible, even obscene. As proof, they would cite Epicurus' claim that 'no pleasure is in itself evil' and that 'we choose the virtues too on account of pleasure and not for their own sake'. I do not wish to argue for either the former or the latter, but will only say that both propositions are taken out of the very broad context of the Epicurean canon, that is, the science of the real world, which includes assumptions and beliefs that assured Epicurus the status of a major philosopher. One of them presumes that the whole of being (*tò pãn*) consists of atoms and the vacuum whose existence enables the atoms to move. Simultaneously, Epicurus held that both atoms and the vacuum had existed and would exist forever. He also assumed that the real world is subject to causal dependencies. Although he did not rule out the existence of other worlds, and even the existence of gods there, he denied them the capacity to interfere in human affairs. Naturally, this has never been acceptable to the followers of religions, who believe in divine powers and their help in solving life's problems. In contrast, such a viewpoint was recognised by some later philosophers and naturalists. During the Age of Enlightenment, Epicureanism was endorsed by, for example, the French philosopher and physician Julien Offray La Mettrie (author of the treatise *The System of Epicurus*, among other things), and the American philosopher and politician Thomas Jefferson (in whose opinion Epicurus' doctrine contained everything that was rational).

It is quite eloquent that neither is mentioned among the great natural scholars who paved the way for the success of the natural sciences today.

Racist assumptions and beliefs

Present-day racism did not appear out of nowhere, pulled suddenly like rabbit out of the hat. Its emergence and ever greater following should be attributed to generations of philosophers, scientists as well as adherents of religions which advocated the exclusion of infidels and atheists. The group of people who adopted racist assumptions and cultivated racist beliefs also included several philosophers and politicians of the Enlightenment era, such as the aforementioned Thomas Jefferson. Although he admitted that black people could be just as brave and willing to take risks as white people, he was simultaneously convinced that they were generally inferior to the latter, both physically and mentally. The nineteenth century saw even more philosophers and scholars who not only presumed that humanity is racially diverse but also believed that the white race is in many respects superior to the members of other races. One of them was the French philosopher Arthur de Gobineau who, in *An Essay on the Inequality of the Human Races* of 1855, distinguished between three races (white, yellow and black), only to claim that the white race had the 'original monopoly on beauty and intelligence', while mixing with other races led to the decline of Western culture and civilisation. In that work, de Gobineau also classifies the Germanic peoples as an Aryan race, to which he attributes the best possible qualities. This line of thought was later followed by other advocates of the racial superiority of the Aryans, such as Georges Vacher de Lapouge. In the 1899 book *The Aryan: His Social Role*, not only did de Lapouge subscribe to the belief in the superiority of this race (represented in his opinion by the South European peasantry) over others but also identified the races which posed the greatest threat (such as the Neapolitan and Andalusian Jews). Similar assumptions and beliefs are formulated in *The Races of Europe* by the American anthropologist William Ripley, and in Madison Grant's *The Passing of the Great Race*; according to American evolutionary biologist and anti-racist Stephen Jay Gould, it is 'the most influential tract of American scientific racism' (cf. *The Mismeasure of Man*).

Those and similar publications offered justification and excuse for the colonial policies of the Western states and the associated slave trade. It is something of a curio that the advocates of racism saw bids to escape as a manifestation of mental illness in the slaves (I refer those interested to the advice given in the mid-nineteenth century to slave owners by the American doctor Samuel A. Cartwright). Another curiosity is portraying North America as a kind of El Dorado for African Americans. In the 1905 book *Man and the Earth*, Nathaniel Shaler – a Harvard geology professor – formulates precisely such beliefs and provides their quasi-scientific justification. However, there were also voices which not only questioned the scientific nature of such notions, but also underscored their adverse social impact, since they exacerbated social tensions and conflicts. Even so, it was only the dramatic events of World War II and the protests of the indigenous population of the European colonies against racial segregation that shook racism so much that today many of its supporters think twice before saying anything to defend it.

Naturally, something that has been part of Western culture for so long cannot be so easily discarded. What renders it particularly difficult is that racism has taken a fairly firm foothold in some Western societies and, on top of that, it has adopted a 'protective colouration' which perhaps no longer affords it an aura of 'sanctity', but at least enables it to retain certain pretence of scientificity. The search for new rationale for racism is exemplified in the work of the American psychologist Richard Lynn. In *IQ and the Wealth of Nations*, Lynn formulates the general thesis that both the poverty and the short stature of the African nations should be attributed to their low IQ. Quasi-scientific, racist assumptions and beliefs may also be found among the supporters of reproductive genetics, such as Nicholas Wade, author of, for example, *A Troublesome Inheritance*.

Some general remarks

The first is directly related to Epicureanism and, indirectly, to those assumptions and beliefs which, although they could not be considered indisputable, became increasingly probable and consolidated their position in science over time. This may be seen with both Epicurean atomism and Epicurean determinism. Today, no one disputes that atoms are not the smallest indivisible particles. On the other hand, it would be difficult to expect Epicurus to devise a correct periodic table of the elements or at least identify the component elements of atoms. Much the same applies to reducing determinism to cause-and-effect relationships. The problem is that such general assumptions do not occur in isolation, but in conjunction with others; equally importantly, they may lead to numerous, distinct conclusions. The former and the latter have continued to raise objections from those who either adopt different premises or at least draw different conclusions. Simultaneously, both sides claim the right to citizenship in science and advance reasons which may and often are the subject of serious dispute; in any case, it would be difficult to consider them utterly unfounded. Consider for instance the debates that took place in 1999 at the American Association for the Advancement of Science. At the time, a modernised version of Epicureanism was argued by Steven Weinberg, an American physicist (Nobel Prize winner for discoveries in the field of elementary particle interactions). Weinberg admitted that there is no – and most likely there will never be – a scientific theory that answers all the important questions about the physical world. However, in his opinion, quantum physics not only enables us to correct the errors and simplifications of the Newtonian mechanics but also explains sufficiently enough that science does not have to resort to faith in a divine planner and creator. The necessity of invoking such a Supreme Being was argued in those debates by the supporters of the so-called Intelligent Design (e.g. the English theologian and physicist John Polkinghorne).

Further remarks concern racist assumptions and beliefs. Drawing on their origins shows that what at first might have seemed fairly naive and innocent, may over time become (as it did) a destructive power not only in the domain of science but also – even above all – in how humans interact with one another. After all, was it not naive of the late seventeenth-century French traveller and naturalist François Bernier to discuss racial diversity according to natural and climatic criteria in *A New Division of the Earth*? Things are not much different in Montesquieu's *The Spirit of the Laws*. The treaty is somewhat comical in that regardless of how one looks at different peoples, nations or races, it always turns out that the French surpassed all other human groups mentally and culturally. However, that naivety and comicality fairly rapidly transitioned into a way of thinking, speaking and acting that denied respect or even compassion to all who were not white or even the whites who lacked the abilities and skills attributed to race of the 'Lords and Masters'. For some racists, those were the Aryans. For others (including contemporary racists in the United States), it means virtually anyone who is white; however, any

WASP is most preferable. Of course, one must weigh one's words – not only when articulating racist or quasi-racist views, but also when assessing those and subsequently propagating such evaluations. In practice, it has never been easy for both ordinary people and numerous scientists who, in genuine 'good faith', are convinced that they are only determining the correlations between the physical and physiological traits and the mental and intellectual characteristics. It is anything but debatable that their more or less explicit racism is embraced by those whose knowledge is informed by what they communicate in quasi-scientific publications.

Agnosticism of scholars

The world of beliefs of peoples at a lower level of civilisation would probably astonish the modern human with its diversity and variety. The beliefs of young children are also abundant and diverse. However, contemporary scientists are expected to call it – as in poker – and either carry out the checks themselves or ask for assistance from those who know the ropes. At least, this is the case with individuals who declare themselves agnostics.

What is agnosticism?

Various scientists will give widely different answers to the question. First, I should perhaps draw on the person who introduced the term into academic circulation. It was first used in 1869 by Thomas H. Huxley (biologist and anthropologist, adherent of Charles Darwin's theory of evolution) at a meeting of the Metaphysical Society to describe a person who 'says he has no means of attaining a scientific knowledge of the unseen world or of the future'. Later, Huxley attempted to clarify the concept by stating that 'agnosticism, in fact, is not a creed, but a method, the essence of which lies in the rigorous application of a single principle. (…) In matters of the intellect, follow your reason as far as it will take you (…) do not pretend that conclusions are certain which are not demonstrated or demonstrable'. Huxley also explained how he arrived at being an agnostic, writing in the 1893 *Essays* that when he 'reached intellectual maturity and began to ask myself whether I was an atheist, a theist, or a pantheist; a materialist or an idealist; a Christian or a freethinker – I found that the more I learned and reflected, the less ready was the answer; until, at last, I came to the conclusion that I had neither art nor part with any of these denominations, except the last. The one thing in which most of these good people were agreed was the one thing in which I differed from them. They were quite sure they had attained a certain "gnosis" – had, more or less successfully, solved the problem of existence; while I was quite sure I had not, and had a pretty strong conviction that the problem was insoluble. (...) So I took thought and invented what I conceived to be the appropriate title of "agnostic." It came into my head as suggestively antithetic to the "gnostic" of Church history, who professed to know so much about the very things of which I was ignorant ...'.

Neither those nor other explanations have put an end to the controversy surrounding the meaning of the term. The distinctions drawn subsequently between various types of agnosticism (one of the more popular ones asserts strong and weak agnosticism) and its later versions would probably not have been endorsed by Huxley (had he been alive). One of those varieties was theistic agnosticism, propounded by Bishop Bernard Iddings Bell, author of *Beyond Agnosticism: Book for Tired Mechanists*, in which such agnosticism is claimed to be a foundation of 'all intelligent Christianity'. That was no particular novelty in science, since an earlier iteration had been espoused by the French philosopher and mathematician Blaise Pascal. Those major discrepancies in how the notion of agnosticism was construed and applied seem to have contributed substantially to its relatively late inclusion in the research on faith and unbelief among scholars, that is, only at the beginning of this century. Those elements were taken into account in, for example, a survey conducted in 2009 by N. Gross and S. Simons at American universities. In that study, 51% of the respondents declared their belief in God, 10% stated that they were atheists, while 13.1% said that they were agnostics. In 2013, Andrzej Gołąb conducted a similar study in Poland, on a sample of 279 scientists with doctoral and postdoctoral degrees. 'The overall rate of believers in God was 56.7% and was highest among chemists (80%), geographers (76.2%), mathematicians and computer scientists (73.1%), and medical scholars (64.5%). (...) 18.3% of the respondents declared themselves atheists, whereas 7.2% defined their stance as agnostic'. The percentage distribution in particular fields and disciplines is different for American scientists. Specifically, according to a survey conducted in 2009 by the Pew Research Centre for the People (RCP) among members of the American Society for the Advancement of Science, the majority of the professed believers are chemists (41%); fewer are found in biology and medical sciences (32%), and even fewer in physics and astronomy (29%). These and other statistical figures do not reflect the internal diversity of belief and unbelief in individual scientists, nor do they account for their motives and reasons. Even so, more detailed questions were indeed asked in the specific studies mentioned here. In the RCP survey, American scientists were asked, for example, about their denominational affiliation; of those scientists who declared their faith, 21% were Protestants and 10% Catholics. In terms of religion, the vast majority of Polish scientists are Catholics, which may be readily inferred given that over 90% of the population are practicing Catholics.

Who is an agnostic?

Nancy K. Frankenberry was one to tackle this question in the book entitled *The Faith of Scientists in Their Own Words*. It presents the views of twenty-one scientists from a range of disciplines, including such celebrities as Charles Darwin, Albert Einstein and Stephen Hawking. Darwin outlined his journey from somewhat naive theism to agnosticism in his *Autobiography*, written between 1876 and 1881, in which he admits having struggled for many years to define his attitude towards religion and his belief in the existence of a personal God. The emergence of the concept of agnosticism enabled him to find his bearings in the matter, as he ultimately recognised that 'the mystery of the beginning of all things is insoluble by us [scholars]'. Consequently, 'I for one must be content to remain an Agnostic. A man who has no assured and ever present belief in the existence of a personal God or of a future existence with retribution and reward (…)'. It is also worth noting that following the allegations of atheism (levelled at him after *On the Origin of Species* came out in 1859) Darwin asserted (in a letter to John Forcyde dated 7 May 1879): 'I have never been an atheist in the sense of denying the existence of a God. – I think that generally (& more and more so as I grow older) but not always, that an agnostic would be the most correct description of my state of mind'. In her commentary on the scholar's intellectual journey to agnosticism, Frankenberry observes that 'the young Darwin received an orthodox Anglican education (…). He firmly believed the Bible to be the inspired word of God'. Meanwhile, Michael White and John Gribbin, the authors of Darwin's biography, claim that during his studies 'he had little time for orthodox Christianity and even less for Anglicanism' but 'he could see that the Church could offer him a comfortable lifestyle and a suitable front to pursue his unabated interest in natural history and entomology'.

Albert Einstein's path was different, not only because he grew up in a different religious environment (orthodox Judaism), but also because he was inspired, among other things, by the writings of a philosopher who, albeit Jewish as well, was an apostate (the Jewish community had in fact excluded him from its ranks). In the Introduction to her book, Frankenberry writes that 'when we come to Einstein, we see the unconventional spirit of a great genius meshing with the intellectual creativity of the Jewish tradition to produce an ardent faith. Einstein's pantheism, like that of Spinoza, whom he admired, was based on a belief in an underlying mathematical intelligence pervading a deterministic universe (…) Einstein could not conceive of a personal God who would directly intervene in the world or influence the actions of individuals or sit in judgement on creatures of His own creation'. Such a perception and description of the scientist's belief and unbelief is supported by the later public and private statements concerning his own faith and the faith of others. He would speak about it so often that after Carl Seelig compiled it, there was enough for a three-volume publication. Some of the observations may be of interest to various people, but they can also be construed and presented in many different ways. For instance, in a letter written in 1916 to Max Born (author of the quantum theory of uncertainty), Einstein notes: 'You believe in the God who plays dice, and I in complete law and order in a world that objectively exists'. This may be seen as an expression of Einstein's conviction that the world is deterministic, leaving no room for the randomness of dice. However, it may also be understood as an attempt to tell God what he can and cannot do. In fact, that was the meaning inferred by the addressee, because he replied: 'Einstein, stop telling God what to do'. More unequivocal views on the existing religions, including Judaism and Christianity, may be found in his other letters, such as the one written on 2 July 1945 to Guy Raner. In the epistle, Einstein denied rumours that a Jesuit priest had converted him from atheism to Catholicism: 'I have never talked to a Jesuit priest in my life, and I am astonished by the audacity to tell such lies about me. From the viewpoint of a Jesuit priest I am, of course, and have always been an atheist'. As Einstein saw it, he 'may be called an agnostic' but he did 'not share the crusading spirit of the professional atheist whose fervour is mostly due to a painful act of liberation from the fetters of religious indoctrination received in youth'. On the other hand, in a letter to Eric Gutkind dated January 1954, he admitted that 'the word God is for me nothing more than the expression and product of human weakness, the Bible a collection of honourable, but still purely primitive, legends which are nevertheless pretty childish. No interpretation [of the Bible], no matter how subtle, can change this for me. For me the Jewish religion like all other religions is an incarnation of the most childish superstition'.

Frankenberry's peculiar gallery of scholars concludes with Ursula Goodenough, retired biology professor at Washington University in St Louis, author of, for example, *The Sacred Depths of Nature*. She may not be as famous as Darwin and Einstein, but the version of agnosticism she advocates deserves some attention. Goodenough sets out with the questions: 'Why is there anything at all, rather than nothing? Where did the laws of physics come from? Why does the universe seem so strange? My response to such questions has been to articulate a covenant with Mystery. Others, of course, prefer to respond with answers, answers that often include a concept of God. These answers are by definition beliefs since they can neither be proven nor refuted. (…) The opportunity to develop personal beliefs in response to questions of ultimacy, including the active decision to hold no Beliefs at all, is central to the human experience. The important part, I believe, is that the open questions be openly encountered. To take the universe on – to ask Why Are Things As They Are? – is to generate the foundation for everything else'. In a sense, these questions open a kind of gateway to the scientists' belief in God and their unbelief. At the same time, searching for answers to those questions is a task they take upon themselves to carry out.

Two more general remarks

The first one is informed by the common notion that the academic community is dominated by atheists. This is neither corroborated by sociological studies conducted in the Western countries, nor by the surveys in Poland. They demonstrate that the opposite is the case, with a clear majority of scholars who opt for various forms of religious faith, including such modalities which do not require the support of ecclesiastical intermediaries between them and their God. The second remark concerns the attitudes towards agnosticism among the scholars who are actually atheists and not only make no secret of it but also advertise it on various occasions. One such atheist is Richard Dawkins, a British evolutionary biologist (former professor at the University of Cambridge). In *The God Delusion*, Dawkins found agnosticism to be an inferior form of theism; it is worse because it tries to pass itself off as science. Edouard Boné expresses a similar view in his book *Dieu: Hypothèse inutile?* [*God: Useless Hypothesis?*] The author draws on a range of scientific theories, including the theory of evolution, and claims that 'the scientist – however they are envisioned – can only explore secondary causes. (...) There are words that are meaningless in their eyes, such as *creation*, *person*, *miracle*. (...) A scientist – being one – cannot invoke the purposive cause in the matters of evolution and life; they are undoubtedly entitled to state the existence of a certain direction, a certain orientation in the development of organisms, but they cannot judge regarding the existence of some original intention'. This declaration of scientificity deserves serious discussion insofar as it would appeal to numerous scientists who have experienced or are experiencing a crisis of religious faith but have not yet reached atheist levels of unbelief (and there is no knowing whether they ever will).

Imitating philosophers

If the importance of philosophers and philosophy could be measured by the number of imitators, they might even be at the top of the ranking. The problem is that imitation may be a strong suit with some while others are markedly worse at it. Sometimes it represents a creative continuation of the philosophies of one's predecessors, but it may be merely a poor copy or caricature as well. Much depends not only on the method of imitation, but also on the thinker who is imitated.

Imitating Socrates

This ancient philosopher is not only considered one of the most significant, but also one of the most influential. He attracted followers even during his lifetime, and for one of them – Plato – this imitation worked so well that the latter became a great philosopher himself. Certainly, one could attempt to define what is so great about Socrates' philosophy that so many have imitated it, and continue to do so today, but it will at best only reflect one facet of that multidimensional figure. At the same time, a universalisation proposition – namely that he was a model of both philosophical thought and practical life for many later generations – is likely to be strongly opposed by those who have mastered the art of writing (Socrates was illiterate) and who are concerned not only about their philosophical cerebrations, but also about satisfying essential needs of their loved ones (Xanthippe, the philosopher's wife, is said to have constantly complained that he neglected his household duties). The attempts to show Socrates' greatness based only on his views appear somewhat more modest. However, they too involve significant corrections, whose authors either admit that they have been made or pretend that they merely pass on the views of their master and preceptor. To a degree, the aforementioned Plato qualifies in the latter group. In *A History of Ancient Philosophy*, Giovanni Reale states for instance that 'the prohibitions of Plato on writing about certain doctrines were not of a purely theoretical character but were rooted in a conviction that was chiefly ethical, educative, and pedagogical, and assimilated from the example of Socrates. Hence it is based on the conviction of the supremacy of the oral expression over the written expression of certain important philosophical doctrines'. Furthermore, 'the followers of Plato were, by now, so far removed from Socrates that they did not feel fundamentally restricted by these convictions, and hence maintained that they could not put into writing anything philosophical, without restriction or limitation. So much more now that the written culture had become the clear victor [...]'.

In the modern times, one of the proofreaders who 'wrote down the entire philosophy'. was the German philosopher Georg W. F. Hegel. In his *Lectures on the History of Philosophy*, Socrates is presented as a philosopher who was a 'pious example of the moral virtues – of wisdom, discretion, temperance, moderation, justice, courage, inflexibility, firm sense of rectitude in relation to tyrants and people; he was equally removed from cupidity and despotism'. His philosophising is supposed to have relied on a dialogue which apparently strove to know 'good as the absolute, and that particularly in relation to actions'. It is at least debatable whether Socrates recognised any absolute in his philosophy. It remains indisputable, however, that Hegel did, and not just any absolute, but the World-Spirit (*Weltgeist*) which he construed as setting out from reason to attain a level of reason that no one and nothing can transcend. It is also indisputable that, as a philosopher and university lecturer (at Jena, Heidelberg and Berlin), he eschewed dialogues with students in favour of monologues in which he spoke from the position of one who already knew everything a philosopher could and should know. In this respect, Hegel does have academic imitators today. The problem is that many of them not only lack Hegel's knowledge of philosophical traditions but also fail at the logic that 'binds' his philosophy into a coherent whole. In any case, one can legitimately doubt whether present-day students expect such knowledge and logic from their lecturers. They attend lectures only occasionally and if they do ask questions in seminars, they concern much more mundane issues than those which interested Hegel.

Imitating Descartes

This particular 'star' of philosophy has faded somewhat today. However, there are still philosophers who – without even invoking Descartes' authority – imitate his philosophical method as well as adopt his general assumptions. One of them presumes that the aim of philosophy is to arrive at a knowledge that is absolutely certain and true. Such knowledge cannot be attained by following the instructions of one's academic teachers (even the best ones), nor by studying the works of philosophers (even the greatest ones). Nonetheless, it may be reached, first of all, by doubting everything that is 'not completely certain and indubitable', as well as obviously false; second, by 'building' one's entire philosophy on what can be defended against that doubt. In the light of his *Meditations on First Philosophy*, one thing which thus stands is 'this proposition: "I am, I exist"', and it does so 'whenever I assert it or think it'. Even so, this is only a starting point for a detailed analysis of everything that belongs to and depends on this *ego cogito*. From Descartes' standpoint, everything that can be called *res cogitans* (thinking things) belongs to it, while the *res extensa* (extended things) are predicated on it. Both the remainder of *Meditations* as well as all his other philosophical treatises were intended to demonstrate that. It should also be noted that in each work Descartes takes a radical stance, seeing either truth or falsehood, certainty or uncertainty, whereby that which has been resolved previously no longer needed to be decided later. He was also firmly convinced that he possessed the intellect and cognitive faculties (such as memory and imagination) that would enable him to avoid mistakes in these judgements.

Even those philosophers who admired Descartes' philosophy and imitated his manner of philosophising to some extent did not share that notion. Already during his lifetime, a number of editors effected such revisions that it was still Cartesian, but now written with a lower-case c. Take, for instance, Henri Le Roy (Regius), a professor at the University of Utrecht, who advanced a physiological interpretation of the Cartesian relationship between body and soul. Several years after Descartes' death (in 1650), Spinoza published his *Principles of Cartesian Philosophy*. Much may be said about Descartes' philosophy, but not that it is a version of theism. On the other hand, Spinozan 'Cartesianism' is commonly referred to as pantheism. In later years, Descartes' philosophy was criticised rather than admired, while those who found a few words of appreciation, confined it to perfunctory and polite remarks. This changed in the late nineteenth and the early twentieth century, that is, during the rise of analytical philosophy. The term is so broad, however, that it encompasses both the understanding conveyed by Rudolf Carnap in the treaty entitled *The Logical Structure of the World*, as well as the framework of logic proposed by Ludwig Wittgenstein in *Tractatus Logico-Philosophicus* (according to whom 'all propositions of logic are generalisations of tautologies, and all generalisations of tautologies are generalisations of logic'). This philosophical formation also includes the Lvov-Warsaw school, represented by the advocate of psychologism, Kazimierz Twardowski, and proponents of various versions of logicism, such as Stanisław Leśniewski, Jan Łukasiewicz, and Alfred Tarski. Kazimierz Ajdukiewicz, professor at the universities of Lvov, Poznań and Warsaw, belonged to the younger generation of that school, while his brand of analytical philosophy is referred to as 'radical conventionalism'. *Pragmatic Logic* by that author served as a textbook of logic at various Polish universities for decades. His fascination with Descartes' philosophy is evinced in the fact that Adjukiewicz (together with his wife Maria) translated *Meditations* from Latin into Polish. I must admit that I also came under the spell of that philosophy during my academic youth (and published a monograph on it in 1980). If I were to say what impressed me most at the time, I would point to the Cartesian radicalism in posing and solving philosophical problems. Today, I do not hold that approach in particular regard.

Imitating Marx

Some may consider it a blasphemy against the philosophical greats to mention Karl Marx in the same breath with Socrates and Descartes. However, I do not put Marx on a par with those philosophers, but follow a sequence, both in terms of chronology and the relationship between their philosophical thought. As regards the question what he took from Socrates, I would just briefly say that he did pay attention to the many mundane problems of everyday life. From Descartes, on the other hand, Marx at least adopted the radical manner of addressing these issues and the deep conviction that the solutions he proposed were the best possible. However, I must admit that at no point in my academic youth did I study Marx, not even his most important works, such as the multi-volume *Capital*, with due seriousness and attention. Had my academic teachers done so? I strongly doubt that, because in the classroom they either told anecdotes or repeated textbook clichés, such as 'capitalist exploitation', 'class struggle', or the final victory of the urban and rural proletariat, who bring the capitalists to a harsh account for their wrongdoings. During the communist era in Poland, there were both Marxists in my academic milieu who took those slogans seriously and there were those who repeated them, but I am not convinced that they made the effort to peruse the writings of their philosophical patron. Either way, neither the former nor the latter registered in any way in the history of Marxism.

Still, certain individuals did contribute more substantially to that respect. Their peculiar 'gallery' may be found, for example, in Leszek Kołakowski's monograph entitled *Główne nurty marksizmu* [*The Principal Currents of Marxism*]. V. Lenin is considered one of the most significant imitators of Marx. Karl Kautsky, representative of the 'German orthodoxy'; Rosa Luxemburg, representative of the 'revolutionary left'; the 'revisionist' Eduard Bernstein, Jean Léon Jaurès, who approached Marxism as a soteriology, Georges Sorel, a proponent of 'Jansenist Marxism', Antonio Labriola, who attempted 'open orthodoxy', Stanisław Brzozowski, who construed Marxism as subjectivism. Chapters in the history of Marxism were also written by those who preached and practiced its 'Soviet' incarnation, which is less a philosophy than an ideology. Here, the list is long, and I will mention only two names by way of example: Leon Trotsky and Joseph Stalin. After World War II, further major Marxist chapters were authored by, among others, György Lukács (who advocated 'reason in the service of dogma'), Lucien Goldman (who did not go 'beyond the standard principles of historical materialism'), and representatives of the Frankfurt School, such as Max Horkheimer and Theodor Wiesengrund-Adorno ('the abundant scholarly output of the Frankfurt School, spans works from the most diverse fields of the humanities …'). One can, of course, argue whether this 'gallery' of Marxists is accurate enough.

At any rate, it must be noted that Kołakowski was well prepared to compile it. Not only was he a critic of Marxism as a mature academic but had also been its ardent supporter in his youth, while *Nurty* … may be seen as an attempt at intellectual reckoning with the 'errors and distortions' of adolescence.

He elucidated what they meant in practice during a lecture delivered at the University of Łódź in 1992, having been awarded an honorary doctorate there. Among other things, he stated that 'when you are twenty or twenty-one, you often think you know everything; I also thought I was all-knowing, and only later I gradually and slowly became more stupid. As that know-it-all, I completely crushed Poincaré's theory, I left him in tatters'. However, Kołakowski 'forgot' to add that, after moving in 1950 from the higher school in Łódź to study at the University of Warsaw, he 'crushed' the *Lectures on the History of Philosophy* by Władysław Tatarkiewicz, in an open letter written with seven other philosophy students. Following the letter, Tatarkiewicz – an expert on philosophical traditions – had his teaching privileges suspended. Karl R. Popper quite aptly observed that the downfall of Marxism was not only due to the erroneous 'prophecies' of Marx and Engels but should also be attributed to the lack of criticism among those who believed and propagated them so zealously that Marxism ultimately became a caricature of what its founding fathers had preached. Even so, I would not argue that, had they not appeared, that philosophy would have defended its rationality before the tribunal of that critical reason which had been born in Western culture as early as Socrates, only to gain ever wider recognition later as it matured and successively rid itself of illusions.

Voltaireanism in academic life

There are figures in Western culture whose thought, speech and acts had an impact on both their contemporaries and the generations that followed. This also applies to their role in academic life. One of those figures is the French philosopher, historian and man of letters, Voltaire.

Historical Voltaireanism

Voltaire was born in 1694 and, until the age of 24, he went by the name of François-Marie Arouet. He adopted the nom de plume in the wake of the scandal after he had accused the regent of incest, which culminated in his imprisonment in the Bastille. Indirectly, this contributed to his reputation as a libertine (free thinker), about whom the biographer René Pomeau noted that he 'was not guilty of showing respect to anything', notably religion which accompanied his entire upbringing and education at the Jesuit College Louis-le-Grand in Paris. The eighteenth century saw many more people who scorned the Christian religion, but Voltaire was different, as he 'was not guilty' of lacking intelligence or literary talents which secured him a prominent position in the history of French literature. From early youth to old age, he poured his reflections onto paper. In effect, his collected works amount to more than fifty volumes. What was the nature of those reflections? A short answer is anything but easy, as he was interested in a variety issues, from strictly scientific quandaries to problems of everyday life that even the uneducated have to confront. Was he an expert on all? This particular question is easier to answer unequivocally. Evidently, not only did he not know everything, but there was no possibility that he would have, if only due to fairly modest education. Still, he supplemented it with self-education and had such a linguistic aptitude that he mastered Italian, Spanish and English on his own. The aforementioned biographer claims that his notions were particularly influenced by the milieu of French libertines who met at Guillaume de Chaulieu's house in Quartier du Temple. At any rate, it is from them that he may have adopted the conviction that the Old Testament is a 'collection of stories and fables', that the apostles were 'naive, gullible idiots', while the Church Fathers were 'charlatans and frauds'.

Even today, such words may be objectionable to both believers and the religiously indifferent who nevertheless have a rough idea of the cultural role of Christianity. Although eighteenth-century Western Europe was religiously divided, it was still predominantly Christian. Aware of this, Voltaire did not assert the above verbatim. However, there are enough of his writings to leave no doubt that he espoused such beliefs. Consequently, the doors of the contemporary universities were closed to Voltaire. They were institutions of religious character and anyone who did not share a particular denomination could neither teach nor study there. Besides universities, various academies of science gained popularity at the time in Western Europe, one of which was the French Academy of Sciences. Was Voltaire eligible to join? Perhaps he was, at least until he published his *Letter on the Academies*, in which he stated that 'in France it is not enough that a man who aspires to the honour of being a member of the Academy, and of receiving the royal stipend, has a love for the sciences; he must at the same time be deeply skilled in them; and is obliged to dispute the seat with competitors who are so much the more formidable as they are fired by a principle of glory, by interest, by the difficulty itself; and by that inflexibility of mind which is generally found in those who devote themselves to that pertinacious study, the mathematics'. Voltaire was not at all keen on such studies, although this did not prevent him from speaking as if he had a sound mathematical background. Obviously, this would not have opened the door to the English academy of sciences – known as the Royal Society of London – to Voltaire either. At the latter institution, the decisive vote was cast by mathematicians and physicists such as Isaac Newton. In the same letter, Voltaire also observed that 'two things, and those the most essential to man, are wanting in the Royal Society of London, I mean rewards and law', himself being particularly 'sensitive' to the former (as a result of skilful market speculation, he had accumulated a considerable fortune). It may also be noted that Voltaire was a master of succinct and venomous retort conveyed in his epigrams. The protagonist in one of those was Pierre Louis de Maupertuis, a highly regarded natural scientist. In the piece (a rhymed quatrain), the author contends that many a tear was shed by the prophet Jeremiah during his lifetime because he predicted the birth of the scholar. That, of course, cemented Voltaire's reputation as a person who had no respect for anyone or anything.

Contemporary Voltaireanism

In secular France, Voltaire is not only present in the names of streets and squares but also features as the patron of quite a few schools. Internationally, his achievements are cultivated and perpetuated by the Voltaire Foundation for Enlightenment Studies, affiliated with the University of Oxford. Among other things, its website informs the visitors that it 'pioneers the methodologies of digital humanities in eighteenth-century scholarship' and that 'the writings of Voltaire and other eighteenth-century scholars were seminal in creating the political and social systems of today. Enlightenment thinkers were champions of rational thought, scientific enquiry, intellectual curiosity, and the separation of Church and State, all of which are more relevant now than ever'. The Foundation's editorial achievements include the *Complete Works of Voltaire*, as well over 600 volumes as part of the series *Oxford University Studies in the Enlightenment* (released with publishing partner Liverpool University Press). In our country, there is the *Racjonalista* website, launched in 2000, 'run by the community of Polish anticlericals, freethinkers and rationalists', and referred to by its creators as the 'Portal of Knowledge and Thought', and the 'De Voltaire Rationalist-Sceptic Centre'. In the last few years, three collections of Voltaire's selected writings have been published in the Biblioteka Kwartalnika Kronos series. Hence, one may confidently say that Voltaire is not just a historical figure but, in a way, continues to be present in contemporary culture.

In the academia, creationists and evolutionists have long been engaged in a major dispute. Both sides have enlisted a substantial number of scientists who represent a range of disciplines and various academic centres around the world. The creationist faction includes not only theologians, but also philosophers and theoretical physicists. Among their opponents, there are evolutionary biologists, philosophers and logicians. However, the approaches of to religious faith are greatly diverse: from those seek a kind of compromise to hardcore advocates of the zero-compromise approach. One of those is evolutionary biologist Richard Dawkins (professor at Oxford University until his retirement in 2008), author of *The God Delusion*. In that book, God of any religious faith is asserted to be a delusion, and religion is a 'dangerous nonsense that teaches enmity towards other people'. Such general propositions are supplemented by various jokes and taunts aimed at creationists, for example, comparing the probability of God creating the world with the probability of the miraculous reassembly of all the parts of a Boeing 737 after it has crashed. In numerous public statements, Dawkins has attempted to demonstrate the irrationality of religious faith in divine creation and the various associated beliefs: that Jesus turned water into wine, walked on water, was born to a virgin, that Mohammed split the moon, that Lazarus was raised from the dead, etc. It follows from a Dawkins' post on Twitter that 'laughter is the appropriate response to such beliefs'. Naturally, it is much easier to laugh at something than to engage in a serious debate with creationists. I do not claim that science should be practiced with funeral-like solemnity. However, one should find the right measure in everything and apply it correctly.

How is Voltaireanism present in our academic reality? There being all too many readers of his numerous works is definitely not a problem today. Indeed, it may even be said that there are relatively few people in Poland who decide to have such a read. However, those who do occasionally familiarise themselves with those writings will readily discover that they all tend towards the same goal, that is, to ridicule the stale religious beliefs and challenge the existing authority, and that they employ the same or very similar rhetorical devices (with saying something 'for' but in fact 'against' at the fore). Even in the works that were given traditional philosophical titles (such as *A Treatise on Metaphysics*), it becomes clear after the first few pages that there is no and there cannot be any room for metaphysics. After all, metaphysics exclusively connoted irrationality for Voltaire. Still, even a cursory perusal of his writings yields a certain lesson: one can reiterate the same thoughts and use the same rhetorical devices and still be considered a great philosopher, a man of letters and an expert on everything that any rationally thinking person should know. Today, the method used by Voltaire to have one's publications 'miraculously' multiply is called 'self-plagiarism'. Call it as you like. It will not bother those who now imitate this relatively simple method of adding to their list of publications, first by turning out a few papers, which are then combined into a monograph, which in its turn is later released in a foreign language, in whole or in part. At each stage, the volume of the output may be increased by 'enriching' particular items with some minor deliberations of the authors. This is also Voltairean.

Likewise, it is Voltairean to claim to be an 'expert', if not on everything then at least on what falls within the scope of the academic discipline in which one has obtained a degree. In an age of narrow academic specialisations, such a person is not taken too seriously in the academia, but in the media, why not? One could even say that there is quite a demand on television for 'faces' who can explain even the most complex problems in a relatively simple fashion, and if they go off the script and start talking too much science, they may expect not being invited in front of the cameras again. I know of an older-generation ethicist who was explicitly told in a farewell interview: 'Professor, what you're saying is too complicated'. Consequently, the platitudes which such academics often say to the camera reflect their ability to adapt to the situation, but at the same time they seriously call their academic degrees into question. In the academic world, there are people who have a congenital need to speak on issues they are not conversant with but on which they have an opinion all the same. If they try to find out more about the subject, fine. Things are much worse when such an individual is unwilling to admit ignorance and speaks with a conviction that needs no explanations; yet, when they receive explanations they have not expected, they are anything but ready to admit shortcomings of knowledge. Obviously, one could simply acknowledge the difference of opinion, but this requires a great deal of self-criticism and the readiness to recognise that others may also have valid reasons to defend their position. Voltaire was 'guilty' of neither the former nor the latter. Is it a fault that may be attributed to present-day scholars who, despite their considerable scientific achievement, have failed to keep up with the advancements in science? They should be the first to answer this difficult question. By way of example, I will only note that it even such a great scientist as Albert Einstein found it difficult to come to terms with it when – as his biographers Roger Highfield and Paul Carter put it – he became a 'priest in the temple' of knowledge; if not scientific, then at least it was knowledge that various types of media have a demand for (according to the aforementioned biographers, Einstein 'owed his sudden fame to the headline writers of newspapers in England and America').

For many years, Voltaire and Voltaireanism have been a kind of intellectual challenge for me. I have spoken and written on the subject repeatedly but invariably there have been questions that I could not fully answer – for myself or others. However, I have never had any doubt that his philosophy is not particularly profound, and that the methods he used to convey his views and judgements have long since been thoroughly and compellingly analysed by experts. Still, the fundamental question remains: what has been the cause of his significant impact on Western culture? The observations advanced here may at best be a contribution in the debate on the topic.

Teamwork or solo?

The eponymous question can be asked in many a profession. The answers will depend on the specifics of the profession and on the changing circumstances that make either teamwork or individual effort more effective at one point or another. Scientific research is no different in that respect.

Profession or vocation?

This question was posed by Max Weber in his 1917 lecture at the University of Munich, which he entitled *Science as a Vocation* (*Wissenschaft als Beruf*). In the critical part, he spoke out against the universities 'developing in the direction of the American system', that is, one in which they operate like any other 'capitalist enterprise', with the 'separation of the worker from the means of production' and the director treating the institute as if it were their property. In the defence part, the lecture called for the university to be treated as if the education it provided were a 'spiritually aristocratic' pursuit, and the research conducted there derived not only from the scholar's 'personal gift' but also from the passion for research that could be construed as a calling. Simultaneously, Weber emphasised that 'no amount of such enthusiasm, however sincere and profound it may be, can compel a problem to yield scientific results. Certainly, enthusiasm is a prerequisite of the "inspiration" which is decisive. Nowadays in circles of youth there is a widespread notion that science has become a problem in calculation, fabricated in laboratories or statistical filing systems just as "in a factory," a calculation involving only the cool intellect and not one's "heart and soul"'. A hundred years ago, these words were merely a warning. Today, they are just an affirmation of the state of affairs at many of the world's leading universities.

Naturally, I do not advocate a style of doing science that yielded significant results in Copernicus' time, that is, when a single scientist working outside the academic environment was able to arrive at great scientific discoveries. Neither am I in favour of science being practiced after the manner of Newton's, who was indeed a university scientist, but owed his most significant achievements to personal passion and courage in questioning many of the erroneous notions in contemporary physics, optics and astronomy. In the nineteenth and the early twentieth century, there were still scientists who carried out research outside the academia that resulted in major success. James P. Joule is one such example. He was a brewer by profession and his investigations into the nature of heat and the relationship between mechanical work and energy was driven in equal measure by a passion for knowledge and the desire to streamline the machinery at the brewery where he started as an ordinary worker to become its manager. In *The Evolution of Physics*, Albert Einstein and Leopold Infeld recall that 'Joule verified by experiment the guess that heat is a form of energy and determined the rate of exchange'. In his research, he used 'a clever alteration' of the weight clock mechanism that enabled him to gauge energy losses. They add that 'it is a strange coincidence that nearly all the fundamental work concerned with the nature of heat was done by non-professional physicists who regarded physics merely as their great hobby'. However, even those who functioned at the time in the academic environment, often had laboratories at their disposal whose equipment far outstripped the then research facilities. This includes the laboratory in which Maria Skłodowska-Curie and her husband Pierre Curie conducted research on radioactivity which won them (together with Antoine H. Becquerel) the 1903 Nobel Prize.

Teamwork

At the time when significant scientific discoveries were made thanks to individual passion and great persistence in delving into issues which posed a formidable intellectual challenge to individual scientists, one of the foremost advantages of teamwork was the need to have one's results evaluated by people who either followed the 'beaten track' or opted for new paths, which nevertheless differed from those that led to correct solutions. Consider, for instance, the seventeenth- and eighteenth-century debates on the nature of light (where the corpuscular and the wave factions clashed). Some of that has endured to this day, but one of the leading benefits of teamwork now is collaboration involving scientists whose specialised qualifications make it possible to solve the multifaceted problems which, although they fall within a specific science, are not covered by a single discipline. This year's Nobel Prize in Medicine and Physiology offers a good example. The accolade was awarded to the American developmental biologist Victor R. Ambros and molecular biologist Gary Ruvkun for their discovery of microRNA (miRNA), 'a class of small RNA molecules that play a key role in regulating gene activity'. In its justification, the Nobel Committee stated that 'the laureates contributed to the unprecedented rate of vaccine development during one of the greatest threats to human health in modern times'. Obviously, this discovery would not have been possible without the laboratory equipment, the financial resources and the group of associates assisting the former at the University of Massachusetts Medical School and the latter at Harvard Medical School in Boston.

While the prestigious award that these scientist received is being celebrated, the public finds out mainly about the benefits of their collaboration, but little is known about the controversies that are inherent to virtually every teamwork. After all, even the most outstanding scientists have their bad days, when impatience and ordinary human exasperation take over, as in the notorious case of the team who discovered DNA (a large organic chemical compound from the group of nucleic acids that acts as a carrier of genetic information in living organisms) in 1953. The team consisted of biochemist and geneticist Francis Crick, biochemist and molecular biologist Maurice H. F. Wilkins, biochemist James D. Watson and laboratory assistant Rosalind Franklin (who earned a doctorate in physical chemistry). In 1962, the first three won the Nobel Prize in Physiology or Medicine for that discovery. J. D. Watson recounted in great detail how that team functioned in *The Double Helix: A Personal Account of the Discovery of the Structure of DNA*. According to Watson, F. Crick was the most colourful character, whom he 'never seen in a modest mood' and who 'often came up with something novel, would become enormously excited, and immediately tell it to anyone who would listen'. On the other hand, R. Franklin appears to have annoyed her colleagues the most, especially Crick ('almost from the moment she arrived in Maurice's lab, they began to upset each other') and Wilkins (she 'would not think of herself as Maurice's assistant'). However one might judge that situation, this was indeed a tremendous great scientific discovery delivered by world-class scientists.

What about the lower echelons of research and the application of its outcomes in practice? I have recently done a 'stint' in a hospital bed. On the walls of the ward where I was staying, there were photographs of both its head of the department and his numerous team. Overall, the people in the pictures seemed satisfied with their professional situation. This is hardly surprising, as it is a university clinic which enjoys a reputation of one of the best in Greater Poland, so getting a mere internship there is unlikely to be easy, while moving up the hierarchy of that team must be even more difficult. I have no reason to complain about the quality of the medical services provided by that team. The approach of individual doctors and support staff towards patients is another matter. I have the best memories of the physician who conducted patient interview with me and immediately passed on his suggestions to the doctor who performed the procedure. In this manner, he helped to shorten my hospital stay by at least a few days. I have less fond memories of how I was treated by the doctor who carried out the relatively simple preliminary tests and who did not seem particularly happy with her position in the hierarchy of the team. It is a well-known fact that the head nurse plays an important role in any hospital department and sometimes you have to be lucky to catch her in a friendly mood. Regrettably, I had no such luck (when it came to being assigned a hospital bed, for example). One way or another, I realised that even the best-organised team includes people who try to highlight their importance.

Individuals and their functioning

Although there is less and less room for the kind of individuals without whom progress in science would not have been possible in the past, this does not mean that significant results cannot be achieved in science while following a solo path. The problem is that the environment of such researchers should recognise their right to do so, as well as allow them to be an individual whose behaviour sometimes deviates from the accepted standards. This tends to vary in practice, even in those sciences whose level of development is considered to be relatively high. A positive example of such a treatment of individual peculiarity is Niels Bohr, the Danish scientist who received the Nobel Prize in 1922 for his 'research into the structure of the atom and the radiation it emitted'. In *Niels Bohr's Times*, Abraham Pais portrays the scientist as someone who 'was able to put his whole being into it and he could convey beautifully how small the point was and how lofty the power', and when 'he was in need of a break in the discussions, [he would] apply himself to the pulling of weeds with what can only be called ferocity'. The author of that biography, who was first a student and later a close associate of the scholar, states that Bohr was 'a man with supreme confidence and a strong sense of destiny, not quite in a hurry but always intensely, perhaps compulsively, engaged in one project or another'. The history of science records Bohr's dispute with A. Einstein over the reality of light quanta (Bohr did not believe that they actually existed) but, as Pais notes, even though they became 'intellectual antagonists, but that in no way diminished their mutual respect and affection'. Such situations happen today as well, not only in highly advanced sciences.

Still, the field of research – even the discipline – is a major factor. Art sciences appear to be the most tolerant of peculiar personalities. The problem lies in the fact that practicing an art science is different from analysing and evaluating that science; furthermore, the applicable assessment criteria are not the same as in the exact or the natural sciences. This specificity is also taken into account in the current official list of scientific fields and disciplines. A considerable degree of indulgence with respect to distinctive individuals is also seen in the humanities, notably in fields such as philosophy, which traditionally draws on the eminent philosophical figures to underpin its 'legitimacy' to be among the academic sciences. Even so, it is one thing to take the best from those individuals and try not to repeat their mistakes, but 'making it' in terms of independence of analysis and evaluation of their achievements is quite another. I learned how difficult this is when reviewing applications in promotion procedures. Not infrequently, persons seeking to become an independent scholar (in our academic realities, this involves obtaining a postdoctoral degree) would submit what was a digest – more or less successful – of other philosophers' views as their principal scholarly achievement. It was passable as long as those were significant and influential philosophers. Once, I had to go through an application in which fairly obscure thinkers were elevated to the main protagonists, while the role of the person pursuing scientific independence consisted chiefly in finding their writings in the archives, translating them into contemporary languages, and providing it all with numerous references to ancillary literature (incidentally, the procedure was successful for the candidate). One also encounters research 'achievements' in which such references are few, but a closer look at the narrative reveals that what is formulated in direct speech is, in fact, either a citation without quotation marks or a paraphrase that differs only little from the original. This, of course, raises serious questions – perhaps not about the scientificity of philosophy, but about the scientific integrity of the philosopher who seeks academic promotion.

Leaders and stragglers in science

While trying to catch up with the leaders in world science, it may be worthwhile to take a look and see who the leaders and the stragglers in this chase group are. This is not always easy. What I have in mind first of all is the situation in Polish science, but the way things stand in the countries we look up to is in many respect similar. They have their exemplary leaders, but stragglers are not lacking either.

The leaders

Regrettably, there is nothing permanent in academic life and being a member of the scholarly community, which is why one has to accept that what used to be good in science a few decades ago may not be very useful today and often is not. This general observation can be supported by specific examples, and leadership in science provides plenty of those. A century ago, it was safe to say that the leaders in science made groundbreaking discoveries and formulated scientific theories whose significance could only be fully appreciated by few. However, those few sufficed to exploit their intellectual potential and 'recast' them into practical applications that terrify some and give others hope for a better future. The list of those leaders is not that short that they may be counted on the fingers of one hand. However, neither is it long enough that they cannot be traced to a specific place and time, or even a particular field or discipline of science. Take, for instance, such biologists as Charles Darwin or physicists such as Albert Einstein. Obviously, such visionaries of science come to the fore even today, but it has become more difficult to distinguish scientific geniuses from those who only consider themselves geniuses or would just like to shine for a while on the scientific firmament, being little concerned that their 'star' will sparkle only briefly and they themselves will end up notorious rather than famous. Either way, it is much easier today to become a 'seasonal star' in science than to continue shining brightly on its celestial sphere for a long time.

The realities of conducting research have also changed substantially. Nowadays, in addition to many more people involved in research, it is also increasingly difficult to achieve significant success in science by working alone or in teams without high-class scientists and international cooperation with acclaimed research centres. Of course, working in large research teams and exchanging scientific experience comes at a high cost. This is another obstacle to be overcome by the scientists who not only aspire to be leaders in science, but who are also adequately qualified, willing to make numerous sacrifices and work extremely hard to accomplish their ambitious goals. And yet, all this is going to be of little use if they receive no support from people who are not and are unlikely to become scientific geniuses in the future. After all, the latter are efficient managers who can raise financial resources where no one else would look or where, even if they happened to 'knock on the right door', it would stay closed. Such people may certainly aspire to the role of leaders as well, as it would be quite 'legitimate' for them to do so, but only in the category of people supporting the scholars who actually carry out scientific research. The problem arises when they not only fail to see the difference between themselves and the scientists whom their management skills are supposed to serve but also elbow their way to the forefront. Besides the various financial awards and honours, they also seek to feature prominently in the scientific publications which communicate the outcomes of collective effort. I do not want to complain yet again about the decline of decorum in science (which would be relatively easy given the domestic realities). To put in a nutshell: at the world's leading research centres that publish multi-author papers (which are the norm in the natural sciences), priority is given to those who have contributed the most to the findings. Any question along the lines of 'what about us?' from the managers involved is answered politely but firmly: they are and probably will be irreplaceable in the future, but their role is and will remain an ancillary one. In practice, this is easier said than done; even explaining to an otherwise distinguished professor that his organisational expertise, and sometimes his name has been and may still be prospectively useful in obtaining funds for scientific research and establishing international contacts is a difficult feat. Indisputably though, the professor's most productive years of research are already over. Meanwhile, taking credit for the achievements of others is, or at least should be, considered reprehensible.

The stragglers

This category of persons in science is also problematic, or at least ambiguous. There are types of stragglers who perhaps do not deserve great recognition, but at least a little fondness and a few kind words. I will cite two such examples. One involves Charles Darwin, whom numerous biologists would not hesitate to recognise as a leader in nineteenth-century science. Even so, it is worth remembering that throughout his adult life, the scientist – outstanding in many respects and bold in his views – was not passionate about the origin of the human and other species (though he ultimately came to the conclusion that the good Lord had nothing to do with it), but about barnacles (molluscs living in the hollows of *concholepas* shells). His biographers, M. White and J. Gribbin, state that Darwin 'thought with delight about studying his beloved barnacles'. Perhaps he should even be acknowledged as a leader in the study of those miniature creatures but given the great significance of the theory of evolution – incontestably a tremendous achievement – those investigations were a waste of time, definitely tantamount to straggling. Another example of a somewhat deserving straggler is taken from Max Weber's 1917 lecture *Science as a Vocation*. Weber describes a scholar who spends his entire professional life analysing a few lines of a historical text and firmly believes that his revised interpretation will not only benefit science but also be salutary to his soul. Naturally, one might say that science – just as any other domain of higher culture – has never lacked individuals whose single-mindedness verged on being 'crazy'. From Darwin's and Weber's standpoint, those kinds of 'craziness' could still mean a small step forward in science, even though they did not lead to a scientific revolution.

Nowadays, science is expected to make big rather than small steps (preferably: here and now). In effect, one shows less tolerance towards the 'crazy' scholars who, oblivious to the expressions of pity or jokes of their close and extended circles, or uninterested in professional accolades, are passionate about such minor problems that only few can appreciate their scientific impact. I do not claim, however, that such scholars are either utterly extinct or that they are a dying breed. In my professional life, I have met several such individuals, though I will not mention any of them by name here. I might only say that I met one such positively 'crazy' person at a time when we were both novice 'academics'. I did not even try to understand the essence of his scientific passion (as he worked in a different discipline), but it was clear to me that he found his research to be more important than academic promotions, for example. Ultimately, however, he also achieved these; today, he is both a full professor and full member of the Polish Academy of Sciences, a scholar respected both at home and abroad. Much more often, though, I could not say anything specific about the interests and achievements of the people I met, but nor could (or wanted) their superiors. In the 1980s, I was employed at one of the research units of the French Centre National de la Recherche Scientifique (CNRS). A certain lady would often speak at the seminar meetings there. When I asked the director of that establishment what that nice lady specialised in, I was told: 'In nothing'. What I wish to say is that such 'experts in nothing' are not found solely in our Polish academic 'backyard', but also at those Western centres that represent the professional dream-come-true of many of our scientists. The difference is that they receive better salaries (whose amounts I will not mention, so as not to dishearten our experts in something); moreover, the stragglers at those institutions are unlikely to have a major impact on the quality of research and the associated standards of academic life. Needless to say, the ratios of experts in quotation marks to genuine experts differ across academic centres, or even within the same centre across various fields and disciplines of science. Even so, the claim that there exist centres and disciplines where there is no room for the former is so implausible that it does not merit serious discussion.

Some general suggestions

First, certain suggestions may be made concerning the presence of leaders in the academic environment. If I were to say that neither did they nor do they currently have such an easy life that everyone would like to imitate them, it would not raise anyone's eyebrows. True, many would like to achieve their scientific success, craving the recognition and the financial resources they receive for their research even more. However, it is not difficult to grasp how much is required in order to become a leader, if not in world science, then at least domestically. If I had to answer – as briefly as possible – what it takes to become a true leader in science, I would go for the right aptitude and qualifications, persistent and effective work, and that bit of luck in life that makes you come across friendly or favourable environments, or at least an environment where our scientific achievement is not perceived as a personal slight or threat to someone's academic position. Apparently, such talents are something one is born with. Even so, they can and should be honed, and the longer and more committed this effort is, the greater the chances of becoming a leader in science. It must be clearly stated, though, that the process demands plenty of patience, not only from the aspiring leaders, but also from their immediate and extended environment. This is not easy for either. Admittedly, it is perfectly normal that some people are more talented, hard-working and intelligent than others, yet it may be irksome that leaders are so much better that the stragglers look like 'poor relations' in comparison. What is worse, these leaders will often not hide that they are superior to their colleagues and co-workers, flaunting the fact on various occasions. That definitely does not make life easier for anyone.

Further suggestions are related to the presence of stragglers in science. I would not expect many to disagree if I said that such a professional modus operandi and their being in the academia is to some degree accepted. The reasons behind it are varied, including more prosaic ones, such as the fact that it is easier to live with stragglers rather than leaders. Not with all and not in every situation, of course. The authors of peer-reviewed publications who had the misfortune of being assessed by a reviewer-straggler would no doubt confirm that this is the case. I could say much about those individuals, not only as an experienced author of such publications, but also as the editor-in-chief of two journals (both are on the ministerial list of ranked journals). However, I will be brief: it is not the duty of such a reviewer to force-find any shortcomings and imperfections in the reviewed books and papers, and to show off what they have recently read or at least have on their bookshelves at home. This does not reflect badly on the assessed texts and their authors, but on the reviewers themselves, who reveal their grievances, prejudices, and occasionally their lack of competence as well. This is particularly evident when such a straggler can be equated with a scientific outsider (which is not so rare). I would qualify the latter as a subgroup of stragglers, though not every straggler may be deemed an academic outsider (as the above examples of eminent scholars show). There was a 'straggler' of the kind in my immediate milieu who, from his early academic youth to late academic old age, kept promising to write a grand piece on pre-Socratic philosophers, which so far has not materialised.

Academic innovations

Calls for some kind of innovation are often heard in the academic community. While some appeals – taken on board and to some extent implemented in practice – are treated as a step in the right direction, it still falls short of what the various innovators expect. Academic conservatism may indeed prove to be one of the obstacles on that path. The problem is that at times it is also a kind of 'lifeline' against innovations that can do more harm than good to academic life.

Cultural changes

Nowadays, people willing to embrace the belief that conservatism is a symptom of a cultural ailment may be found without difficulty. Multiple generations of innovators of all sorts have laboured for conservatism to be perceived and presented as such. Particular contribution should be attributed to the representatives of Enlightenment, who helped create a world of cultural values and greatnesses in which human reason, liberated from the errors of the past, and human resourcefulness, no longer encumbered by the 'shackles' of traditional beliefs, reign supreme. The assessments of that period will naturally vary, but there is no doubt that it witnessed a major confrontation between the 'old' and the new world. It is also evident that the latter emerged victorious from the clash – it was not as easy or quick as various innovators would have liked, yet they finally managed to strip the conservatives of their socially significant positions. The anticlericalism of the nineteenth century and the twentieth-century democratisation of social life in the Western countries were a kind of 'overtime' that clinched the showdown in between the forces of the 'old' and new world. Again, this did not go without a hitch, either. Moreover, that period saw the rise of such social forces as communism which, under the banner of building a new and better world, actually meant a return to the 'old' world in which 'the only right science' and 'the only legitimate authority' have a right to exist.

Regrettably, the question of what it all brought forth and what has taken root in contemporary culture cannot be answered conclusively, since much depends on the point of view. To the supporters of modernism, many Western countries saw the emergence of cultural pluralism, which meant social acceptance of diversity and difference of belief, custom, morale etc. The so-called postmodernists go even further in this respect, talking about 'liquid modernity', 'liquid truth', 'liquid morality' and many other such 'liquidities', meaning that what used to be considered a value only yesterday can be and often is less valuable today, only to become so worthless tomorrow that 'crossing swords' over it is futile. Conversely, the defenders of the fading world see it as cultural destabilisation, which causes even well-educated people to lose their bearings, having no clear direction to follow. In *After Virtue*, one of such defenders, Alasdair MacIntyre, compares this to a ship in stormy seas about to capsize, as it lacks both a proper captain and the right navigational tools. The question of how this translates into education in a modern country like the United States was answered by Allan Bloom in *The Closing of the American Mind*. In the subtitle, the author promises to show and demonstrate 'how higher education has failed democracy and impoverished the souls of today's students'. Those cultural 'liquidities' affect contemporary science as well, though I am not saying that they are always harmful. However, I share the opinion of those scholars who, like the co-authors of the book *Pseudoscience. The Conspiracy Against Science* (Cambridge 2018), believe that they usher in a variety of pseudosciences.

Unwholesome innovations

I am going to cite only one example of such pernicious innovation (though I could name more, of course). The phenomenon is not confined to the academic life in Poland, but that is no excuse, even though it would be legitimate to say that the disease has reached us in the wake of infatuation with

Western culture. However, I will not follow the approach adopted by any of the authors cited here when discussing that complaint. After all, we have our homegrown innovators, who admit having contributed to the law adopted in 2018, known as the Constitution for Science or Act 2.0. Its provisions have been translated into the statutory regulations at public universities and are implemented with varying degrees of success. Now, what I consider a sign of unwholesome innovation is the commercialisation of scientific research which, in short, prioritises the resulting material output or hard cash, and preferably both. This is something new because, as Kazimierz Twardowski noted in 1932 in his lecture *On the Dignity of the University*, one of its foremost traditions is 'the pursuit of scientific truths and probabilities as well as nurturing the ability of inquiry' and, secondly, 'the awakening and deepening in young minds of an understanding of the enormous significance that objective truth has for humanity'. It might even be that the co-authors of Act 2.0 were familiar with that lecture or at least were aware of the dangers that giving precedence to the 'market' poses for academic life. However, it appears that either they were out of their depth given the scale of the problem, or they simply downplayed it. Be that as it may, the provisions of that law offer hardly any remedy for that disease. For the proponents of the mercantile approach to science, talking about a vocation to attain knowledge is, in fact, either some old-fashioned twaddle or simply a waste of time. In any case, they find no issue with such terms as 'human capital' or 'commercialisation of knowledge'. The problem is that such capital can be generated not only by conducting truly scientific research, but also by what merely disguises itself as research, but in fact has little to do with science. The aforementioned commercialisation can just as easily mean selling rubbish and something with actual scientific value. Incidentally, rubbish often sells better than genuine knowledge, as the popularity of various types of pseudoscience in the mass media clearly shows.

One of the corollaries of this unwholesome innovation is commercialisation of scientific journals. Naturally, some of them publish more scientifically valuable articles than others, but for a large proportion the chief goal is financial gain of their founders and owners. Certain journals are so aggressive in their pursuit of lucre as to be called 'predatory'. They regularly advertise their publishing services also to Polish academics, and I think it fit to cite an example of an offer that I received recently. I will not disclose the name of the journal (so as not to give it publicity) but will only mention that having one's religious studies paper published costs a 'bargain' price of CHF 1,200. It is a monthly with several dozen articles featured in each issue. No matter how you count it, this translates into substantial profit for its founders and owners, though it does not mean that the Polish authors reap no benefits from publishing their papers there. The journal is on the ministerial list of ranked periodicals, with a high score at that. Needless to say, being placed on such a list also requires a lot of effort from the editors, but they have their ways and means. One of them is to set up a 'publishing cooperative' (often under an academic banner) and enhance the impact factor (IF) by referencing their own or 'friendly' journals in the bibliography. The authors also have to be involved, and it is likely that more than one has received an 'offer you cannot refuse' from the editors, that is, to add an assortment of suggested items to the references in their paper. It is not that that the very creation of journal lists or publication databases such as Scopus (which many of our bibliometrists consider an oracle) is unwholesome. However, I argue that it would be worthwhile to revise such lists every now and then and take a serious look at the database, as it can be fallible (at any rate, it does not really present a picture of health today).

Healthy conservatism

I could cite numerous examples of that healthy conservatism in academic life. Naturally, the degree of impact that they have on how the academic community delivers it tasks tends to vary, but I would not underestimate any of them. By way of example, I will refer to the conservatism which manifests in academic ritualism, such as wearing gowns and birettas or giving speeches in Latin at ceremonial occasions. Not only does it have a certain charm but also contributes to the integration of the community. Even so, neither charm nor integration will 'feed' academic science and teaching (if one could speak of the driving force of research and student education in that fashion). I see much greater impetus in the desire of scientists to achieve significant academic success and to climb the ladder of academic hierarchy. It would be fine if the latter were a consequence of the former, but it has never been easy, whether in the past or today. At least, it was easier in the past to tell the difference between the master, the journeyman and the mere apprentice in the academic profession. A hierarchy of the kind is also seen today in academic life, where formally there is a person with a master's degree at the lowest level, followed by one with a doctorate slightly higher, then a postdoc at an even higher level, and the professor at the top. However, this is only a formal hierarchy, because in reality both lower- and top-tier academics often lack something to become truly excellent. The opinion of Maciej Żylicz (former reviewer of professorship applications to be signed by the president) should offer much food for thought to those who think about improving academic life in Poland. Żylicz noted that many a candidate for professor had such poor academic credentials that they should not even have obtained a doctorate; and yet, they were awarded the title of professor. This is only possible in the age of 'liquid modernity', in which nothing is taken literally and seriously. If a fundamental change of that attitude is not feasible at the moment, we should perhaps start by limiting the possibility of demonstrating it so frequently.

Admittedly, the co-authors and proponents of the Act 2.0 have adopted that particular course. This is reflected for instance in the provisions which stipulate the appointment of four (instead of three, as was the case previously) reviewers in the postdoctoral procedure, and the reinstatement of the postdoctoral examination in the humanities and social sciences. Also, other sections make it obligatory to have five (formerly four) reviewers in the procedure culminating in the award of professorship. In either case, none of the reviewers may be from the same university where the candidate for the degree or title is employed. The establishment of the Council for Scientific Excellence (to replace the Central Commission for Academic Degrees and Title), and the introduction of the rule that reviewers are drawn from a group of at least ten experts in a given discipline are also indicative of the intention behind the law. For the time being, it remains uncertain whether this will generally improve the situation in promotion procedures. Still, it would be legitimate to say (based e.g. on the number of rejected professorship applications) that some progress has been made.

For my part, I would suggest going much further, without confining ourselves to promotion procedures or devising such criteria of scientific achievement as publishing with ranked publishers and journals from the ministerial list. Evaluation of grant applications is definitely an area which requires treatment. Here, the ailment manifests in a situation when the applications are reviewed by persons whose achievements are perhaps known to their closest colleagues but remain rather obscure to the broader scientific community. Another symptom of the malady are promotion procedure panels whose members demonstrate much more modest scientific achievement then the candidates they assess. Even if they do not act in the capacity of reviewers, their status on the panel entitles them to a vote – whether to grant or reject such an application – which counts just as much. I believe that taking such steps is necessary, though there is no doubt that it will be difficult to carry it through. After all, if no attempts are made to remedy those situations, there is no chance for a healthier life, while it is only natural that the healed complain of other ailments that have not yet been treated.

Academic weigh-ins of the professor and the student

The results of the weigh-in will invariably depend on who or what is weighed, but the measure also plays a paramount part. This is not much of a problem in the standard procedures, but becomes one in the case of academic weigh-ins. For one thing, they employ certain peculiar measures, yet the central issue is that we are dealing with people who may be worth an investment of time and money. All the same, a closer look is required to see if, by any chance, they are not 'cheating' on the scales.

The weigh-in of the professor

It is an academic tradition to see professors as figures who carry the most weight. In the early centuries of universities, the equivalent title was that of *magister* (Lat. *master*). In many countries, that particular tradition has been upheld but the weight attributed to professors may vary. At least two major types may be distinguished, the first of which I would call the British model. However, it may be encountered not only in the UK, but also in other European countries and at selected American universities. Its characteristic feature is the limited number of professorship types. At the old English universities – such as Oxford or Cambridge – there is only one title and one position of professor, which constitutes the crowning and pinnacle of one's academic career. It is awarded to persons with outstanding track record in terms of research, and the remuneration is higher than for the lower-grade university positions (of a reader, for instance). There is usually also only one type of professorship at the more recently established universities, but it also happens to be merely an honorary title at quite a few. The formal thresholds at both old and new universities are determined by the universities themselves. In the US, on the other hand, one finds several types of professorships (e.g. assistant professor, professor of practice, or research professor), while at the most prestigious universities there (such as Harvard), the solutions in this respect are not unlike the British model. The stratification of professorships in Germany is not that different either, as it features a division into three classes, that is, C2, C3 and C4. The latter denotes the highest rank: a professor who besides major scientific achievement heads a chair or a department.

The second model may be called Romanesque, since it is primarily seen at universities in France, Italy and Spain, but as the countries choose to follow their own paths, the diversity of the professorship structure increases. In France, the title of professor is not only given to university faculty, but also to secondary school teachers. University professors, on the other hand, are divided into three classes, the third (highest) of which is divided into two levels (*échelons*), the second into three levels and the last into six. There is also the position of associate professor (*professeur associé*). In Spain, professors are divided into three categories, from A to C, with C being the lowest tier in the hierarchy. This position is also open to persons without a doctorate. There are also assistant professor, associate professor and temporary professor positions at Spanish universities. Only those with significant academic achievement and at least three years of academic experience as a category B professor can apply for the highest professorship (category A).

In Poland, the professorship model resembled the British one for many years, with only two types, that is, associate and full professorship. This changed in 1990 and, while the title of professor was retained, the positions at public higher schools included both university as well as full professorship. The former position is available to persons with a postdoctoral degree but without the title of professor. Moreover, one can have the status of a visiting professor at Polish universities, for which persons with at least a doctoral degree may apply. The universities themselves are empowered to determine specific requirements that the candidates for professorships must meet. They are fairly strict at some schools (e.g. the Jagiellonian University) and relatively liberal at others (Adam Mickiewicz University, for instance). However, the latter approach is more common, which means that next to the abundance of postdocs, university professors proliferate as well.

If this were accompanied by the kind of scholarly quality that would put them on a par with the professors at major Western universities, we would not only catch up with the West but even outdo it.

The weigh-in of the student

Although it varies across the Western countries, the most important dividing line runs between those where studies are paid for by the student or donors who provide them with financial support, and the countries where their education is publicly funded. The former includes the United States and the United Kingdom. The majority of European countries, on the other hand, are in the latter category. Still, this does not mean that there are no other indicators and gauges on the relevant scales. In the most elite universities, such as Cambridge and Oxford, the tuition fees are high but so are the requirements thanks to which one can select a relatively small group of students who will be able meet the educational demands. On the other hand, in the countries where the taxpayer covers the cost of higher education, the selection 'sieve' is often in the hands of the minister, who may but does not have to approve a certain major at a university, even less an admission quota that would cost much but turn out graduates for whom there is no social demand. Occasionally, the demand actually exists, but the universities have insufficient staff to provide instruction at an academic level. This is the case, for example, with psychology, a major which has long enjoyed considerable popularity.

Every year, a record number of secondary school graduates apply to enrol for psychology at my former university (AMU). The university authorities made efforts to tackle this educational challenge, but even the most resourceful administrators cannot miraculously increase the number of psychologists with academic qualifications who can deliver the core curriculum. However, the problem has to be dealt with somehow. Before the watershed of 1989, one such solution was to apply the criterion of social background (preferably working class, but peasant origin was acceptable as well). Afterwards, admission has been decided based on grades on the secondary school certificate and the so-called enrolment interview. Though it has not helped to 'patch up' the staffing gap, one can turn away the vast majority of applicants who fare worse at the preliminary selection process than the relatively few lucky ones. The former are not left to fend for themselves, however. The relatively large number of private universities in Poland will welcome at least some of them with open arms – as long as they can afford to pay the tuition fees, of course. The amounts these schools charge are dictated by the market, that is, the higher the number of people interested in studying there, the higher the fees. These private institutions are also able to cope with staff shortages, too. It may be difficult to train their own faculty, but there have never been any major obstacles to 'filching' them from public universities, offering primary or secondary employment. During the education boom of the 1990s, there were lecturers who managed several additional jobs at private higher schools, often hundreds of kilometres apart. Today, that 'onslaught' of secondary school graduates at the gates of universities has significantly abated, but the fashionable programmes registered only minor decline in applications.

The student weigh-ins at some ecclesiastical universities deserves some mention, particularly given the quite notorious story of a student who was refused admission because he did not have the right certificate from his parish priest. That revealed a much broader and deeper problem, as it concerns – to a greater or lesser extent – all universities operating under the supervision of various Churches. I would expect that it manifests differently depending on the higher school in question. However, in each case, it is handled not only by the rectors of such institutions, but also by their ecclesiastical superiors. While I do not wish to add fuel to the already heated debate about the 'priest's certificate', I have the impression that the issue is particularly complex for the theological faculties established at secular public universities after the 1989 transition. They are subject to twofold authority, that is, the competent bishop and the rector, whereby the former has the right – even the duty – to guard the students' conscience, whereas the latter would put not only the student, but also themselves in an awkward position if they were to enforce the conscience clause. The fact that so many people drop out of theology programmes after the first year is something to ponder for both superiors. Although in this matter I rely only on data from my university, I assume that things at other faculties of theology are not much better.

In 2017, Student Staff Ratio (SSR) was introduced as a weight measure applicable at public universities in Poland. In 'officialese', SSR is a quality-focused index of availability of scientific-teaching and teaching staff for academic instruction; in plain language it reflects the ratio of students per capita of such a staff member. For universities that receive public funding (now called a subsidy), the weighted average should not exceed thirteen students, and ten students at the higher schools which aspire to the status of research university. The term weighted average is used because it refers to the university as a whole and not to individual programmes. A university which fails to reach this ratio will suffer negative financial consequences in the shape of decreased ministerial subsidy. In fact, such consequences were discussed at a meeting of the Adam Mickiewicz University Senate in which I participated. According to the calculations supplied by the rector's office, even decimal values, that is, about a quarter of a student, would translate into millions with such a large institutions as the AMU. Although the university is not far from having thirteen students per lecturer, the ratio is substantially exceeded in some programmes while others fall well short of it. It is easier to tackle the excess than the shortage. According to the rectorate, the solution to the first problem was to 'raise the score threshold for admission to bachelor's degree programmes, tighten the rules on resuming studies and transfers from other universities, consider the possibility of abandoning continuous exam sessions, limit admission quotas in selected fields of study, and discontinue ineffective programmes'. However, I did not hear the authorities advance any idea of how to solve the long-standing scarcity of applicants willing to enrol for programmes which had had trouble filling the quota for years. A radical solution would be to discontinue such programmes altogether. However, next to the highly qualified personnel who are employed to teach there, those programmes are the ones that the university a university.

So far, students have not been all too concerned about the SSR index. In any case, I am convinced that only a few know what it means or even that it exists. Perhaps they should be advised of the fact on some occasion, especially in majors where it is significantly exceeded. After all, it might mean that they will face a 'slaughter of the innocents' even in their first year of study. So far, the university authorities have not decided on such drastic measures for the psychology programme. At the faculty of law, however, this has been practiced for years, and law students may even be surprised that there were so many of them in their first year and far fewer later on. Still, such problems affect those higher schools in Poland which receive numerous applications each year, despite the demographic low and the diminished prestige of university studies. What about those universities which fight for each secondary school graduate only to strive to keep those who have enrolled as students and pay tuition as long as possible? Today, such a situation is faced by many private higher schools which, during the education boom, had to rent large auditoriums to be able to hold lectures. I do not have any good advice for those universities, while saying that it is 'time to pack up' is unlikely to make any of them happy.

Academic decency

There are probably many people willing to agree that it is better to be decent in life rather than not. For some, though, bothering about it is a waste of time, because people have different understandings of decency anyway. Indeed, it would be difficult for me to define what decency means in a mere few words. However, one can consult various guides, including those dedicated to decency standards in a particular community.

The guides

Looking for what the word decency means, once can obviously consult Google, but even that source of all sorts of knowledge does not offer an easy solution to the linguistic quandary. It does provide a long list of both synonyms and antonyms, and even groups them according to meaning and context, but while this may be helpful for some, it may create an additional obstacle for others. After all, questions of decency are usually concerned with specific behaviours that will go together with certain dictionary synonyms and antonyms, but the people asking them expect unequivocal rather than ambiguous answers. Ambiguity in this respect can be and often does serve as a kind of excuse for those who consider decency an anachronism or a 'voice in the wilderness' that deserves no response.

Regrettably, the academic community does not seem to fare much better when tackling this linguistic ambiguity. In a sense, this is corroborated by the *Code of Ethics for Scholars*, for instance. In this document, drafted by the Commission for Ethics in Science, the term *decency* is not mentioned even once, but a number of its synonyms and antonyms are enumerated instead. The preamble already refers to the modes of conduct that scientists should follow, namely 'respect for human dignity and life in all its manifestations, truthfulness, integrity, the duty to honour accepted obligations, and recognition of the right to freedom of belief and ownership'. All of these may be considered synonymous with decency. On the other hand, Section 3 of the Preamble speaks of what qualifies as antonyms of decency: 'the recently intensifying practices of courtesy reviews, plagiarism, holding multiple positions, unjustified citation of works and exploitation of the resources of the institutions in which one works for one's own ends'. The section of the *Code* entitled *Good Research Practice* mentions such manifestations of decency as 'conscientiousness in presenting the aims and intentions of intended or ongoing research', 'credibility in conducting research', 'not using one's scholarly authority when speaking on issues outside one's scope of competence', and 'independence from external influence on the conduct of research'. Further, the section entitled *Non-Compliance in Scientific Research* states the most blatant manifestations of indecency: 'fabricating research results and presenting them as true', 'altering or omitting inconvenient data', and 'committing plagiarism'. Although the document is quite well known to the academic community, it needs to be recalled from time to time, as new infringements against decency in its midst come to light. For instance, its provisions were recently referred to in issue 4/2020 of the Polish Academy of Sciences quarterly *Nauka*. I am convinced that the editor-in-chief of the magazine, Jerzy Brzeziński, would not have opted for such a reminder had he not thought that things were not going well with decency in academic life, to the extent that a warning 'red light' should be turned on.

Departures from decency

Next to the aforementioned Code, instances of such departures are often cited by scholars, whether online or in community magazines, such as *Forum Akademickie*. The latter has long featured a column entitled *From the Archives of Scientific Dishonesty*, while its author, Marek Wroński, does not appear to be running short of material for the series. I have also spoken on this matter more than on one occasion. The only reason why I invoke it is to answer why I choose to focus at this point on one single problem, that is, the official lists of scientific journals and peer-reviewed materials from scientific conferences that the ministry publishes with some regularity. I do not claim that most of the journals on the list and the score they have been assigned attest to a departure from academic decency. However, I do not make such a claim primarily because I do not have the competence to substantively evaluate over 31,000 items on the list, but simultaneously I seriously doubt whether the co-authors of those lists were adequately competent as well. Similar misgivings are expressed by others who comment on this issue, but their astonishment or even indignation are not directed at all the titles but – first as foremost – at those that owe their high scores to the so-called predatory practices and predatory ministry officials. Such periodicals are relatively most numerous in the fields of humanities, social sciences and theology. I feel more competent in this area, especially with the journals that have been (more or less accurately) classified within the humanities. After all, I have been conducting research in this field for several decades, and I am familiar with the milieu-specific and scholarly realities of the persons involved in those disciplines. I know many of them personally or as authors of papers submitted for publication in one of the journals of which I am the editor-in-chief.

I will start with the latter journals. Both have featured on all the lists of scientific periodicals issued at various times and even obtained higher scores in the later ones. Deservedly? I can say with full conviction that this is the case, because they have gradually improved in terms of regularity of publication and the range of works by scholars from various academic centres. However, as regards their being on a par with the so-called leading Western journals, I can say with equal conviction that there is still a lot of work to be done. All the same, in my opinion, their scientific and editorial quality is by no means inferior to many of the listed journals with a higher score. This is where the decency issue rears its head, as noted by the numerous critics of the list. Some of the periodicals elevated to an indecently high rank remain obscure to most of the academic community, and if they happen to be known, it is mainly in local or church circles. In certain cases, the rating of the journal was so high it may have even come as a surprise to its editors and the authors, but they hardly protested the fact and certainly enjoyed it. The situation is relatively clear for the journals included the Scopus database, which some scholars revere as an ultimate authority of sorts. Still, the problem is that next to journals which enjoy an excellent reputation in the milieu due to superior quality of papers, it also includes periodicals with which the amounts charged for publication are a priority. As for Polish journals, financial issues are also important, but somewhat less significant; at any rate, their editors have not (so far) been that pushy in demanding fees as their foreign counterparts.

The defenders of such lists claim that many Polish journals make a 'unique, positive and one-of-a-kind contribution to the development of given fields of knowledge in Polish science', as well as seek to prevent 'certain fields of knowledge practiced in the country from dying out, so that they may serve the Polish nation'. Of course, it is debatable whether these criteria were formulated aptly enough to ensure that the journals rated so highly on the ministry lists will actually serve Polish science and the Polish nation well. One can also dispute whether adding them – 'out of the ministerial hat' – to so many other Polish journals, which often took place without consulting the designated body, formerly known as the Committee and later the Commission for the Evaluation of Science (KEN), does not violate applicable laws. At least the frame of reference for the decency to which the ministry and their advisors subscribe, is known. We also know what KEN draws on in the Official Statement which expresses 'concern over the publication of a list of ranked journals in which numerous items have not been consulted with KEN'.

A handful of suggestions

One could, of course, say that the revisions to the list of journals are the proverbial 'fly in the ointment', but this is what critics of the changes will be inclined to say. On the other hand, their advocates will probably maintain that the previous list of journals is nowhere near 'ointment', and they are not entirely wrong, because it was fairly widely criticised as well. One could, and indeed should, ask whether it is possible to draw up a list of ranked scientific journals that would not affront common decency (in its entirety or where it really counts). At least some of the critical voices in the debate suggest that there are scholars who believe that science does not need such lists at all, and that there is a range of more objective criteria to determine high-quality research and significant outcomes. However, even they have to concede that the matter of who should establish such criteria and decide whether they apply in academic life remains in contention.

In fact, that particular question is raised in the polemics between the authors and defenders of the ministerial lists and their critics. According to the former, the casting vote belongs to the Minister of Science, given that the ministry issues the list. Conversely, the latter argue that the final decision should rest with a representative body of the academic community, such as the KEN. There is no doubt in my mind that each of those ministers pursued the policy of the parliamentary majority, but scientists and science are not the primary concern of such policies, as the ministry openly admits. This is not to say that science should be left to scientists alone, but I would nevertheless claim that if politicians have to be involved, those who do it best tend to have considerable scientific experience in addition to political competence (whereby that experience has been gained not only in their own academic 'backyard', but also through participation in international academic life). The critics of the list maintain that the vast majority of those appointed to the position lacked such experience. This naturally begs the question why they were appointed in the first place? I have my opinion on this matter and, though I will not advertise it here, I am convinced that it is not an isolated one. I also have my own opinion on the academic expertise of at least some members of the KEN, including persons who assess scientific journals and determine their scores. I have expressed it both in *Forum Akademickie* and the *Nauka* quarterly. I am not going to mention any names but will only say that I share the view that has been repeatedly voiced in the debate, namely that the KEN has gone too far in one direction (I would call it 'pumping up the balloon' of bibliometric indices accepted by its members). On the other hand, the lists' proofreaders at the ministry went over the top the other way, pushing for the national, milieu-specific and denominational direction. However, 'swinging to and fro' is this manner does not benefit serious science and serious scientists. Naturally, they are able to weather it while doing their job and caring little about the ranking. And this what most probably will happen in this case.

There is still one question I find compelling, though I do not expect to receive an honest and open answer, as it could overshadow the supposed success of certain periodicals that have shot up the list. Nevertheless, I am going to ask it. Specifically, do the editors of the journals that have made this quantum leap in score feel anything where their sense of decency is concerned. Do they mind being on an online 'blacklist' of those who have been given much more than they deserve? Hopefully, at least some of them have mixed feelings, but I would not bet much on them being in the majority. Hence, let me therefore conclude on a somewhat philosophical note: in life (including academic life), nothing is permanent, while short-term successes can both build a better future and ruin what has been built with so much effort over the years. So what should be done? In my opinion, we should just carry on doing our thing and avoid worrying too much about the people in academic life whose incompetence does more harm than good.

The temptation of the scholar

Everyone has been and is exposed to various kinds of temptations in their lives – including those who are listed in the church's list of saints. Today's scholars are not expected to merit joining this group by their behaviour. They are expected, however, not to succumb too much to those temptations that lead them away from scientific research and educating students. The list of these temptations is very diverse, and some are easier, while others are more difficult to overcome.

On temptation allegorically

It is often more apt to speak allegorically about something as sensitive and touchy as temptations than in specifics. This was especially the case in art, and some works were and are so eloquent that they can be an introduction to the titular problem. One of the most suggestive is the triptych by the Dutch painter Hieronymus Bosch, entitled: *The Temptation of St Anthony*. It later inspired other artists to present their versions of the temptation of this saint and has not only been translated into several painted versions, but also into a novel (by Gustave Flaubert) and a film. Bosch's triptych, interpreted 'catechetically', expresses such cardinal sins as: pride, greed, impurity, envy, and immoderation in eating and drinking. The temptations presented allegorically in it can also be translated into those that a scholar encounters in his professional and private life. They do not usually take the form of devils with horns, or that winged bird that devours newly hatched chicks, or even, rarely, those whores who tempt with their feminine charms. However, they do take the form that may seem unthreatening to less experienced scholars, and more experienced scholars may no longer have enough faith in the possibility of facing them. It is therefore worth mentioning at least those temptations that should be faced – if, of course, one wants to get to scientific 'heaven'. For the most ambitious scholars, it may be making a breakthrough discovery in science, while for the slightly less ambitious, it may already be finding oneself at the top of that academic hierarchy, the highest level of which is designated by the title of professor. I am inclined to risk the statement that the former is available only to those who are not only exceptionally hard-working, but also exceptionally talented. On the other hand, the latter is also available to those who are able to make up for their lack of talents with diligence.

Tempting a young scholar

Although some members of the academic community can sometimes be said to be 'born scholars', this is at best a nice compliment that can only be taken seriously by those who are poorly versed in the realities of this life. These are usually young scholars who are only at the beginning of their academic path to gaining increasingly higher professional qualifications and more significant positions in the academic environment. The vision of reaching the top can be compared to St Anthony's desire to find himself in that heaven in which Christians believe. However, there are few who believe that it will be easy. It is no different with young scholars. Assigning them above-average talents can be both a facilitation and a hindrance. It can be a facilitation in obtaining the status of a member of the academic community. However, it can be a hindrance when they treat such nice words as sufficient legitimisation to abandon efforts to improve their abilities. In extreme cases, they can make them so proud that 'holy God won't help' – not to mention pleas to come to their senses. Did this happen to those scholars who have significant achievements in science? It is difficult to answer this question unequivocally. However, we know a lot not only about their difficulties in adolescence, but also about those teachers who did not 'pamper' them with compliments. An example is the outstanding mathematician Hermann Minkowski, who was Albert Einstein's teacher in high school. He remembered his student as a person who stood out, but not in the field of mathematics – in which he was supposedly an '*imbecile*'. There is much to suggest that this was an unfair opinion. However, it can be treated as evidence of Minkowski's use of the so-called cold upbringing – if one can say that this is how one encourages students to work on themselves by pointing out various kinds of shortcomings and imperfections. Of course, one must be careful with this, because one can easily become like the bird in Bosch's painting that devours its chicks. However, Einstein's upbringing did not do much harm to his intellectual development.

His love affairs and disappointments have also been described in considerable detail not only by biographers, but also by himself in his extensive correspondence to family and friends. On this basis, we can say that from an early age he was sensitive to female charms. However, this was not the kind of 'sensitivity' that translates into harassment of female and male students by academic teachers. It takes place in various countries and sometimes takes on such proportions that it is widely publicised and commented on in the media. In the United States, according to a report based on research conducted in colleges in May 2005, 18 percent of female students received e-mails of erotic content, 7 percent encountered attempts to remove their clothes, and 5 percent were offered better grades by their lecturers in exchange for sex. In Poland, at the beginning of 2025, the case of one of the deans of the University of Warsaw, whose sexual behaviour towards students and colleagues caused outrage and indignation, became widely publicised. Of course, it is not only young scholars who are involved in this behaviour. However, in this age group, it is particularly difficult to determine the boundary between ordinary advances and harassment, and to indicate the initiating party. I would not like this to be understood as an excuse for those who believe that youth has its rights and that it is worth having a little sexual fun before male and female charms cease to be so captivating that few people will be impressed by them. However, the temptation to think this way is sometimes so great that such a young scholar begins to perceive students as 'game' and himself as a hunter entitled to hunt.

A good opportunity for such a hunt may be his feasting with students – especially when it is accompanied by alcohol consumption. Its abuse by some members of the academic community was and still is a serious problem (although it is rarely talked about openly). Although this temptation rarely looks as impressive as in Bosch's painting, even with a much more modest arrangement you can drink and get so drunk that later older students tell younger ones about it, and graduates recall it with amusement at friendly meetings after many years. Of course, I am not saying that a scholar should be such a 'saint' who refuses to drink alcohol in every situation. Even if they are, they have to explain to their environment such rare abstinence. Either way, the problem is not so much not to drink alcohol, but not to get so attached to it that you can no longer live without it, and with it you can not only somehow survive a hangover but also stay in academic life. However, it is important to have a so-called strong head not only for alcohol, but also for hiding this addiction. However, it helps few people to achieve good results in scientific research and in educating students. If you do not have it, then all that is left is to count on the understanding of the academic environment. Sometimes, however, you can miscalculate this. I know one case of such a young scientist. I know more scientists who, despite their weakness for alcohol, survived in it until retirement, and even went through the entire academic path from student to titular professor in it.

Tempting a mature scholar

The age of a scientist may or may not indicate crossing the boundary between youth and maturity. What's more, it can be misleading – especially in those areas of life where so much depends on individual talents and the desire to develop them. These include not only science, but in science these differences are relatively clearly visible. The problem is that today's scientists rarely want to look like (with apologies) St Anthony, who appears four times in Bosch's triptych, that is, like an old man dressed in a monk's habit with a cane. Besides, he rarely looks like that. More often, as if time was late in leaving its mark on him, and if it has already left its mark, he tends to hide it under the mask of youthful behaviour or at least dressing (without a tie, of course). This is not yet a sin, and it can improve the scientist's well-being. Either way, the temptation is great – especially when such a mature scholar wants to impress younger colleagues with his appearance and behaviour at social gatherings. At least in the American academic environment, such behaviour is met with a lot of tolerance.

However, more credible certificates of maturity are also expected there – not only scientific, but also personal. It can be expressed in the fact that research problems are undertaken, the solution of which does not exceed the intellectual abilities of the scientist, and the possibilities of the research equipment at their disposal. If the former are present, but the latter is lacking, then one can look for a better place for scientific activity. This often happens in the United States, and for now, it gives such good results in scientific research that the universities there attract many scientists from other countries like a magnet. However, there are relatively few universities in this country that conduct scientific research at a high level. There are, however, many that deal mainly with educating students. Receiving a job offer or even an internship at a prestigious university requires not only presenting an interesting research plan, but also a CV that includes significant research achievements, documented by publications in important journals and publications. It is easier to receive such an offer from universities that focus on teaching, and easiest from organisations that support the international exchange of academic staff. More than one Polish scientist has taken advantage of such an offer. It also has its advantages – but mainly in the case of those who are just starting their academic career. However, there is also a danger that such stays in foreign centres will constitute a 'spreading' of the research potential that promising scientists have. For those who do not have it, they are only a kind of sightseeing tour. I have also met such 'tourists' during my stays in foreign academic centres.

A mature scientist usually has a stable financial situation, including financial. Of course, it varies not only in different countries, but also in the same country, and even at the same university. The measure of his maturity is not so much that he would not like to improve it (there are few such people even among Christian saints), but that he would like to improve it without harming the scientific research he is conducting. One such possibility is to prepare a research project and submit it to a competition for a research grant. The problem is that there are many such originators, and relatively few awarded grants. What is more, there are relatively few that involve large financial resources. The temptation to receive them is so great, however, that the ranks of those applying for them do not tend to decrease. At most, some losers in such competitions replace others. There are also scholars who take the saying literally: 'let the living not lose hope' and repeatedly line up in the same queue for these financial resources. Sometimes this turns out to be a good solution, because those who evaluate their applications are different and what in the opinion of some does not deserve recognition, in the opinion of others turns out to deserve distinction. I know the case of such a notorious grantee who was and is very successful in this field, because only in subsequent awards did he come across favourable opinionators. Of course, you can find other ways to improve your financial situation. In our country, such a method that enjoys considerable recognition in the academic community was, and to some extent still is, taking up employment in an additional place of work. Although today the possibilities of finding it in a university other than the one that is the primary place of work are smaller, because there are fewer people willing to undertake academic studies than in the 90s of the last century, still many private universities have a large number of academic teachers 'borrowed' from public universities on their staff lists. More ambitious scientists, however, aim to improve their financial situation by first obtaining a postdoctoral degree and then the title of professor. The first one means not only a significant reclassification on the list of university positions, but also on the salary list, including those related to performing managerial functions. Obtaining the title of professor improves the financial situation to a greater extent, but it is within the reach of relatively few.

The profane in academic life

If higher schools are – or at least aspire to be – temples of knowledge, they must be prepared to confront the profane who may come to question their sanctity. Still, besides the fact that this sanctity is debatable, the role of such profane figures in science and academic teaching is also a matter of contention. Some happen to contribute to its development, while others hinder it.

A little history

For many centuries, the boundaries between the sanctity of academic science and the sanctities of the Church were fluid, and those involved in the former could not disregard the latter. Naturally, some scholars navigated this balance better than others – as evidenced by notorious cases such as Galileo's trial. There were also those who accepted the dogmas of faith but defied ecclesiastical interference into their research. If, in addition, they were bold enough to voice this publicly, they had little hope of being inducted into the academic community, whereas if they were admitted by some 'miracle', their academic life was anything but easy. After all, until the mid-nineteenth century, universities were largely religious institutions, which meant that entry was granted only to those who at least declared to share the faith of the Church under whose patronage the school functioned. In the eighteenth century, this brought about not so much a deep crisis in science but caused a significant decline of several once-prominent European universities. The scholars for whom there was no place at such institutions sought refuge in dissenting schools, such as the Warrington Academy in Cheshire, where Joseph Priestley, a pioneer in research into electricity and chemical compounds (discoverer of e.g. nitrogen, oxygen, ammonia, sulphur dioxide and hydrochloride), taught modern languages and rhetoric. While the nineteenth century saw major changes in England, its two flagship universities – Cambridge and Oxford – underwent substantial reforms only in its latter half, albeit not to the extent of allowing the 'profane' theories that defied the belief in the divine origins of man, such as Charles Darwin's theory of evolution, to be taught there. Much the same happened at many universities across continental Europe.

In the twentieth century, many universities established at the time embraced a mission best summarised by Kazimierz Twardowski in his lecture *On the Dignity of the University*: 'to pursue truths and scientific probabilities and to cultivate the skills of attaining those'. That was not a particular novelty, echoing the creed of the universities founded in the late eleventh and early twelfth century. This is explicitly recalled in the *Magna Charta Universitatum*, promulgated in 1988 to mark the 900th anniversary of the University of Bologna. The difference was that the pursuit and the cultivation no longer took heed of what various Churches had to say about those truths. Also, universities gave precedence to what became known as academic freedoms. Article 3 of *Fundamental Principles* in the *Charter* states that 'freedom in research and training is the fundamental principle of university life, and governments and universities, each as far as in them lies, must ensure respect for this fundamental requirement'. Naturally, the freedom and the respect fared variously in practice, even in the countries such as the United States, whose universities have 'hogged' the top places in the prestigious Shanghai Ranking. This was because 'players' who bet either on ideology or profit entered the 'game' for the minds and conscience of scholars. The former won big stakes in the communist and fascist states, while the latter continue to succeed in the democratic countries. In the United States, even the most prestigious universities, such as Harvard, operate primarily with financial considerations in mind. Of course, this does not always mean a profanation of academic sanctities.

The major players

Wherever the game for the 'rule of minds' has been taking place, the institution which held the reins of power would become the dominant players. Historically, this meant royal and ecclesiastical authorities. In *Intellectuals in the Middle Ages*, Jacques Le Goff describes the struggle of universities to assert their rights, highlighting the threats resulting from the ascendancy of either local bishops or the royal sovereign. Those universities which managed to evade episcopal jurisdiction often fell into the grip of the monarchs who 'sought to lay their hands on corporations which brought wealth and prestige to their kingdoms, and which formed breeding-grounds out of which their officers and functionaries would come'. They benefited only when the power-holders were familiar enough with academic life so as not to behave like bulls in a china shop. Queen Elizabeth I of England is often cited as such a ruler, as her reign was a heyday for Cambridge and Oxford. However, kings or queens of the kind were exceptions rather than the rule. If asked whether much has changed in this regard today, I would struggle to answer. I might not know their qualifications, but this is not the issue; it is observation of their actions that causes the problem. After all, there have been government ministers with academic degrees and titles, and yet their decisions have rarely been well received by the majority of the academic community. Quite recently, the ministry was headed by a person with a background in law, who even held a postdoctoral degree, but their actions were approved by few while causing outrage among many members of the academic community.

Today, the biggest players – not only where the battle for the university is concerned – do not reside in Warsaw but have their offices in Brussels. I would expect that most officials there have academic backgrounds, and some may even have the experience of both studying and working at a university. The problem is that they are just greater or lesser cogs in the vast machine of Brussels bureaucracy which – as any bureaucracy – has its advantages and shortcomings. As Max Weber noted in *Economy and Society*, one of its assets is 'hierarchical organisation of authority', whereas the former includes 'entrenchment of the right to office', filling positions 'without concern for the patents of education' and 'hiding its knowledge and action from criticism' as well as possible. In effect, the most important role in such bureaucratic institutions belongs to the officials whose competence, or lack thereof, determines the handling of any affair, no matter how simple. So far, European universities have not reached the level of bureaucratisation seen with their American counterparts. However, if Europe continues blindly imitating the States, it is not inconceivable that academic degrees and titles may soon lose their significance. Meanwhile, we are going to see the rise of such grand titles as university president, member of the board of trustees or executive board, which includes both persons with substantial academic expertise and those who have none, but have successfully managed businesses and advised on the financial and development policies of a university. In Poland, there have already been attempts – more or less effective – to operate in line with that model. While establishing university councils outside financial expenditure is relatively harmless, even beneficial in some cases, deprecating postdoctoral degrees and professorial titles raises serious concerns about the future of academic life.

The minor players

Recently, a higher school which made the headlines in Poland was Varsovia – Collegium Humanum, a non-public business and applied sciences university. Its administration took the schools name literally, focusing not only on business education but also on profiting from diplomas which were sometimes conferred upon receiving bribes. Among the graduates were politicians from various parties and individuals seeking qualifications to secure positions in state-owned companies. I do not claim that all have obtained their diplomas fraudulently, but it is difficult to distinguish between those who actually studied and passed their exams and those who merely paid for the degrees. Moreover, Central Anti-Corruption Bureau has also detained the rector of the University of Social Sciences and Economics Sciences in Gdańsk, the rector and founder of the University of Applied Sciences in Wrocław, and a professor at the Jagiellonian Academy in Toruń following allegations of multiple acts of bribery involving members of the Polish Accreditation Committee. There are serious grounds to wonder whether potential corruption practices have taken place at other higher schools. After all, the mercantile approach has been widespread at numerous non-public institutions which sprouted like mushrooms in the 1990s, while their presence on the educational market does not rely on the highly qualified faculty, but on fees. Charging tuition for higher education is not necessarily tantamount to desecration of the academic sanctities. After all, in countries such as the US and UK fees are a standard and, at least at some universities, the substantial tuition amounts do translate into first-class education. The real profanation occurs when higher schools operate to generate profit by providing opportunities to obtain a degree, luring the students who can afford it through clever marketing. At one point, I collaborated quite closely with a private higher school, whose actual owner had no major academic experience, but possessed such managerial skills that several thousand students attended the school at the height of its popularity, taught largely by the staff from public universities. This 'borrowing' of the faculty was so common at the time that some lecturers exploited the skill of travelling around the country to share their knowledge at several private universities. Not infrequently, their academic profession was thus profaned, especially when they appeared at meetings with students which resembled mass rallies rather than academic lectures.

The catalogue of the profane in the academic milieu is even broader, as it also includes individuals who add their names to the work of their subordinates. Admittedly, more and more people dare to speak out about it, but the actual extent of the problem remains unknown, particularly at those universities where individuals who genuinely contribute to science have little say in the matter of promotions and remuneration. Those who claim credit for the scientific achievement of others also qualify among the profane. Such cases have long been exposed in *Forum Akademickie*. Occasionally, the plagiarists are stripped of their degrees and professorial titles, as well as lose their university positions. Finally, there are those who commit outright crimes but, until proven guilty in court, they need to be presumed innocent. Moreover, they cannot be expelled from the academic community, while legal proceedings culminating in a conviction often take years, allowing them to remain in the academic community despite serious allegations. For several years, I sat on the rector's committee for anti-discrimination, which examined cases where the victim and the aggressor could be relatively unequivocally identified, as well as cases where neither party was blameless. Although the members of the committee would opine that such aggressive behaviour is unworthy of a scholar, the rector could at best give the aggressors a reprimand and put it on record. The aggressive statements concerning the realities of academic life that appear in various periodicals are an even more complex affair. Their authors may at times have some understanding of those realities, but not enough to distinguish between what is a lawful, common practice and what constitutes a breach of the law. The problem is that such contrived abuses reinforce the conviction among the public that there is nothing sacred about the academia. And yet, this is not generally the case.

Academic opinion-giving

Academic life provides so many opportunities to act as an opinion-giver that few members of this community have not acted in such a capacity. Of course, some perform better in that role, others a little worse, and still others do it in a manner which begs the question who even entrusted them with the task. This is because such reviews say more about the opinion-giver's wanting competence than about the value of the achievements under review. However, they are often taken seriously and have an impact on the professional situation of those reviewed.

Promotion procedures

Throughout the several decades of being in the academia, I have both undergone repeated assessments by various types of reviewers and drafted opinions as part of various promotion and publication procedures. Quite a lot has changed in that time, both in terms of rules that govern reviewer appointments and their accountability when discharging such duties. However, if I were to answer whether the current provisions and their enforcement have thoroughly eliminated the involvement of opinion-givers who are incompetent or simply focus on finding fault with the work of the reviewee, I would seriously hesitate to state so. Still, I am inclined to agree that they have to some degree curbed the kind of pathology in the milieu as appointing 'bespoke' reviewers. In some cases, this meant anticipating a decidedly positive opinion, or a decidedly negative one in others. In theory, selecting such reviewers has never been particularly difficult, since the academic community generally has a fairly good idea of whom to call upon for an opinion. It has become more difficult today, because at least in promotion procedures the reviewers are 'drawn by a computer', if being randomly chosen from a group of experts in a given scientific discipline may be thus called. Even so, someone has to collate such a list. Moreover, there are so few high-calibre experts in certain fields that others have to be added to the list, though only if their qualifications are approached somewhat liberally. It is still fine if such an opinion-giver tries to cover up their inadequate qualifications with generalised assessments and doubts. On the other hand, it is much worse if – in spite of these shortcomings – they formulate unequivocally negative evaluations. Also, the outcomes of the procedure may be considerably influenced by the mere members of the academic degree or title panel, since they are entitled to voice their opinion when discussing the application, and to participate when its rejection or admission to further stages is voted. Essentially, they are not expected to double for the reviewers who, on top of that, will introduce significant corrections to the opinions of the latter. The fact that they sometimes aspire to such a role and even decide to write a negative opinion on the achievements of a candidate for a postdoctoral degree or professorial title may be both a testimony to an error in reviewer appointment and an expression of their desire to seize the opportunity (perhaps the only one in their lives) to shine on the academic stage. Albeit not very often, I have encountered such cases, nonetheless.

Still, it must also be said that those with the actual competence and authority to pass opinions in such procedures confront the Hamletic question: to be or not to be an opinion-giver? The statutory provisions state that this is an academic duty. Admittedly, it may be refused, but only in those special instances where conflict of interest, professional dependence or family connections are involved. Also, it is possible to interpret these provisions in a manner that the conflict is more apparent rather than real. This does not mean, however, that a person appointed as the reviewer can in no way refuse to write an opinion and is only left to draft a definitely negative assessment. A scarce handful are devoid of what may be called charity, and there are even fewer individuals willing to assume the role of the 'executioner' to strike down the candidates who are unable to meet the requirements of a degree or title, much as they would like to. In promotion procedures, a particularly difficult situation is faced by the reviewers who personally know the candidate and sometimes even owe them some debt of gratitude. No matter how one looks at it, its repayment cannot and should not manifest in turning a blind eye to substantive and formal shortcomings of one's work, not to mention such borrowings from other scholars that, even with a very flexible approach to copyright, cannot be regarded as original output. Much might be said about such plagiarists, but also about those who, at least until the malpractice has been determined, assess the scientific achievements of such persons positively. The latter are most likely more numerous than those who were caught committing plagiarism and had their names made public.

Publishing procedures

I feel I am entitled to speak on the subject because, first, I have written many an opinion of the kind, and second, I have several decades' worth of experience as editor-in-chief with a publishing house specialising in peer-reviewed scientific monographs (included in the ministerial list of such publishers). Plus, for several years now, I have been the editor-in-chief of two scientific journals (also on the aforementioned list). The time and effort it take to review a monograph and a paper is not the only difference; work on the former can be and usually is paid, whereas no remuneration should be involved with the latter, at least formally. Consequently, the approaches of the reviewers differ as well, but not to the extent which would warrant saying that the assessment of the monographs submitted for publication are generally much more thorough and substantive than it is the case with papers. On more than one occasion, the publishing house I headed received monograph reviews which were as brief as they were general, while any critical remarks were concerned with secondary or even marginal issues. From time to time, however, we would also receive very extensive and detailed opinions which, by and large, culminated in a negative conclusion or at least recommended thorough amendments. There is a notion in the academic community that it is much easier to write assessments which conclude positively rather than draft negative ones, since the latter require a more exhaustive rationale. There is something to it, indeed, but this is not always the case, as I have also come across monograph reviews in which the negative conclusion was not conscientiously justified, giving the impression that author had not bothered to read the content carefully. Perhaps they had only leafed through it, or even confined themselves to reading the table of contents and the passages which interested them a little, as well as looking over the items cited in the bibliography. The ensuing negative evaluation of the monograph might to some degree stem from the fact that the reviewer did not find any of their works there. After all, there is nothing wrong with wanting to be appreciated or at least to be cited often enough for the impact factor to be high, though treating it as the most important – if not the only – indicator of a scholar's standing is debatable. On the other hand, it remains indisputable that the wounded ambition of an opinion-giver does not sufficiently justify their negative opinion concerning the scientific value of the monograph under review.

This problem is also seen – on an even larger scale – with the assessments of papers submitted for publication. Theoretically, becoming thoroughly acquainted with their content and the background aspects does not demand such a substantial amount of work that experts in a given discipline or field should refuse to undertake it or fail to carry it out with a diligence which raises no objections from both the authors and the editors of the journals that requested the opinion. In practice, however, this diligence varies greatly. Naturally, some reviews have the relevant components marked in the review form (with a 'yes' or 'no'), and their author also completes the fields under the headings 'evaluation justification' or 'reviewer's comments'. In a proportion of reviews, only the necessary boxes are ticked and, what is more, no trace of the reviewer's work can be found in the text itself either. In such a situation, one can reasonably doubt whether they actually took the trouble to read it. After all, it is difficult to believe that they have been presented with a text that is perfect in every respect. At any rate, as regards the journals of which I am editor-in-chief, we find that such reviews do not offer sufficient grounds for the article to be accepted, and discontinue to use the 'services' of such reviewers. The assessments whose authors have clearly either had a bad day or simply have some kind of grudge against the authors of the reviewed texts are also a major problem. Of course, the texts submitted for review should be and usually are anonymised, but if scientific interests and achievements of their authors are widely known, they are recognised without too much difficulty by the reviewers, including those for whom writing a negative review is a good opportunity to settle the score for one thing or another. Unfortunately, editors of scientific periodicals are hardly ever in the know of the circumstances which give rise to these 'bitter grievances'.

If they knew them, they would probably prevent any 'getting even' with the authors of the assessed papers. Where publishing reviews are concerned, these paybacks tend to vary. Sometimes, such a reviewer even goes to considerable lengths to demonstrate the incompetence of the author. Sometimes, however, they only make the effort of looking for significant flaws and, not having found any, they treat very minor items (such as a misplaced comma or a term they do not understand) as grounds enough to state that the article contains linguistic errors and its author fails to use scientific language correctly (I have seen such a 'review' more than once).

Self-proclaimed 'opinion-givers'

It should go without saying that no one is born a consummate reviewer, and it takes a lot of time and effort to achieve perfection. The fact that there are such 'opinion-givers' in the academia who have empowered themselves to voice an opinion on the achievements of their close and more distant scholarly milieu and do so on various occasions does not make it any easier. Worse still, they sometimes garner recognition in the community. They may be encountered in different age groups and at different levels of the academic hierarchy. It is not too bad if they are young and – science-wise – barely 'fledged' PhDs who pass positive or negative opinions about their peers. Not infrequently, however, they venture well beyond that, sometimes parroting opinions heard from their scientific superiors and mentors, and sometimes articulating their 'own view', which nevertheless is not supported by either adequate qualifications or even thorough knowledge of what they are appraising. The higher such self-proclaimed 'opinion-givers' stand in the academic hierarchy, the more seriously their opinions may be taken – and often are. Occasionally, they happen to be quite highly qualified, though their expertise does not always overlap with the specialty of the reviewee. If animosities in the milieu come into play as well (and it is impossible to avoid them altogether), such 'opinion-givers' will not soil their hands with what their opponents have written. They simply know that the latter are incapable of any significant scholarly achievement and communicated in a serious monograph or paper, while if they have already published something of the sort, they will maintain that it was either a minor publication or that its authors have benefited from overindulgence of the publishing reviewers.

During the relatively long period of functioning in an academic environment, I have had to deal with such self-proclaimed 'opinion-givers' on multiple occasions. One was an extreme case: for an independent academic, his list of his publications was astonishingly short (especially given the many years spent at the university), but his opinions of others were highly condescending, even though they could boast an extensive body of publications and other academic accomplishments. As he saw it, they may have been fairly prolific, but their works were essentially scientifically worthless. Somehow, he did not seem to catch on to the fact that his name did not feature among the scientists whose publishing output was posted for everyone to see on my faculty's website. Today, such a list can be found on my university's homepage. Obviously, this does not make life easier for such self-appointed 'opinion-givers', but it would be overly optimistic to expect that they will stop coming forward to express their personal 'for' or 'against'.

Academic expertosis

The eponymous expertosis was diagnosed at one point by a team of experts and described (e.g. in *Forum Akademickie* No. 4/2014) as one of the disease entities of the academic environment. However, it was presented as a 'poor sister' of pointosis, or at least its questionable 'charms' were not sufficiently highlighted. Undeservedly, in my opinion, because not only does it have a longer tradition than pointosis, but also its manifestations are no less compelling. Fortunately, there have always been academics who believe that it should be treated rather than courted.

The traditions of expertosis

Its traditions go back to the distant times when the first philosophers appeared and began to speak as if they were experts on everything. No ancient philosopher could count on wider recognition among his contemporaries (let alone being remembered by later generations) if he had publicly admitted that he did not know this or that, and he would have certainly been ostracised and lose esteem if he had revealed that he really knew nothing. Although Socrates' 'I know that I know nothing' went down in history, it was not only an intellectual provocation, but also an inducement to find out whether someone actually knew something or knew nothing. Socrates' knowledge was tested by both his students and his rivals in the pursuit of philosophical fame, and it not infrequently turned out that despite knowing something indeed, he still had a lot to learn in order to be deemed a credible expert on life's crucial issues.

Philosophers found themselves in a particularly difficult situation when the Augustinian creed of 'believe so that you understand it' had taken hold. It was not just any faith, but one whose praise was proclaimed by the authorities of Christianity. In the Middle Ages, they gradually gained a leading position, at least in terms of the faith and knowledge preached from the heights of church pulpits and university lecterns. Those who dared to question their infallibility often found themselves in serious trouble. The late twelfth century saw the establishment of an ecclesiastical institution called *Inquisitio haereticae pravitatis* (known since 1542 as the Congregation of the Roman and Universal Inquisition), whose task was to track down and prosecute those whose thoughts and words raised suspicion that they did not follow the instructions of church experts. Various secular authorities also felt entitled to dictate what was and was not appropriate in public discourse, issuing decrees (as was the case during the reign of Elizabeth I in England) not only against the 'riotous and dissolute' life of students, but also against 'their abusive vociferation'. While much has changed since then, not only in the Church (the Inquisition was transformed in 1908 into the Supreme Sacred Congregation of the Holy Office, which in 1965 became the Dicastery for the Doctrine of the Faith), but also at the top of the secular power. Still, tradition does its part and, from time to time, there are individuals in both ecclesiastical and lay positions who are convinced that they know best what and who has the right to think and speak, and where they may do so. These notions are not always shared by people they would like to win over, whereas in the matters considered fundamental by scholars, the competence of such church and secular authorities will invariably be openly challenged.

Contemporary expertosis

The claim that various experts today have it harder than in the past is not particularly tenable. After all, they currently enjoy particularly favourable conditions to proliferate, speak publicly and decide what is and what is not right or proper. I do not mean the so-called media pundits alone (although this is a serious problem as well), but also experts in the various spheres of academic life, including reviewers in promotion and grant procedures, or advisors to political and administrative decision-makers. Today, it may even prove difficult to find a reasonably 'fledged' academic who has not acted in the capacity of an expert somewhere. To a degree, this is understandable because academic life has grown more intense and, at the same time, it has retained its hierarchical structure; consequently, in order to move up the hierarchy, one's professional achievement must be evaluated by those who have already reached the next level. Naturally, this does not apply only to the promotion procedure itself, but also to many prior procedures which involve opinion-giving, for instance when seeking to communicate the results of one's research in scientific publications acknowledged by the experts to be important and reputable, or when applying for funds for research projects with various grant-giving institutions. Both cases offer much scope for the genuine and the so-called experts to be active. I have commented more extensively on the aspirations and qualifications of the latter in *Nauka. Kwartalnik PAN*, in the article entitled *Zastąpić Pana Boga?* [*Replacing God?*]. However, I cannot say with absolute certainty that nothing has changed since then. The question is whether it has changed for the better or for the worse.

That being said, I do not wish to be labelled as someone who just nitpicks and cannot see the big picture. Therefore, I will address the big picture in terms of the role of experts on the Council for Scientific Excellence, a state body established by the Act 2.0 to 'promote the development of scientific personnel'. The internet offers interesting examples of the decisions taken by the Council's praesidium concerning the award of professorships, where the opinions of most experts appointed to assess the merits of the application were positive, but the verdict of its eleven members was negative. It needs to be noted that this committee is composed of persons who represent various academic fields and disciplines, whereas the title is only conferred in one field, with a specific discipline also being stated. Obviously, it could be that the experts appointed at earlier stages of the proceedings had been incorrectly selected. In this procedure, the experts are suggested by the representatives of a given discipline in the field section and selected at random from a pool of fifteen candidates. I also happen to have been thus selected as an expert and have to admit that my company included scholars with whose scientific achievement I was familiar and those I had not heard of before. Their names, of course, are irrelevant, because the individuals are not the problem – the big picture is. No matter how one views such a mode of appointing experts, it is still better than the previous approach. At this point, however, I need to name certain specific disciplines, as expertosis is more widespread in some then it is in others. According to publicly available information, during the reign of the late Central Commission for Academic Degrees and Title, there were some confirmed experts capable of processing an astonishing number of promotion applications. The first place belonged to linguistics and its two representatives: one was an expert 113 times over three terms of office, while the other served in that capacity 100 times over two terms of office. Not far behind were the two leaders in political sciences, one of whom returned as expert 100 times over three terms of office, while the other did so ninety-five times. Two representatives of philosophy came next, with the first one being involved in 'mere' sixty-six promotion procedures during three terms of office, while the second one handled 63 (in his 'defence', he needed only two terms of office to manage that). The diligence and commitment of those experts in the work of increasing the ranks of academic staff may of course be admired. On the other hand, one can also wonder how varied one's qualifications must be in order to take on that responsible role given the vast scope of inquiry within these disciplines. Naturally, I am not saying that any of these experts did not possess the necessary qualifications or that they were insufficient. The only question is whether anyone assessed it and was actually able to do so? There is also something eloquent in the fact that the existence of the Central Commission was terminated, ending the 'misery' of the experts who had to toil appraising scientific achievements in which they were less than well versed.

Remedial measures

Steps to remedy the situation are also being taken today. Some of them are intended to appeal to the academic conscience and to encourage people not to think exclusively of themselves but also consider the needs of the entire academic community; the other may come as a shock to scholars. One of the propitious measures is the *Code of Ethics for Scholars*, drafted by the Committee for Ethics in Science. In a commentary on the *Code* published in *Forum Akademickie*, the chair of the committee, Andrzej Zoll, claims that it was 'based on the ethical principles that apply in every civilised society'. The preamble to the *Code* enumerates the virtues that should guide every scholar, such as 'reliability, integrity, credibility, objectivity, impartiality and independence'. Chapter 5 (*The academic as an opinion-giver*) and Chapter 6

(*The academic as an expert*) directly address the issue of experts and expert opinions. Among other things, the former highlights such reprehensible practices as drafting 'perfunctory, courteous and malicious' opinions ('Such opinions not only cause harm, but also severely impair the authority of science in the society and undermine the community's right to self-governance'). The latter stipulates for instance that 'a scientist shall undertake to prepare an expert opinion or part thereof only within the scope of their specialisation', and goes on to state that while doing so 'they shall not be influenced by the expectations of the principal and shall not allow the principal's pressure to affect the substantive content of the expert opinion', and that 'they shall refuse to prepare an expert opinion whose parts and final conclusions may be associated with their personal interest'. Lofty words, one could say. However, there would be no need to utter them and include them in the *Code* if such reprehensible conduct did not occur among scientists or if it were a marginal occurrence.

The comments concerning various types of experts and expert opinions in science posted on diverse online forums often deviate radically from that loftiness. A proportion would qualify as hate speech and therefore do not deserve to be taken seriously. However, I believe that some are an important voice on major issues relating to the realities of academic life. In my opinion, this includes the critical commentaries – whether posted on online discussion forums or featured in community periodicals – concerning the ministerial list of scientific journals and publishers of peer-reviewed monographs. There have been many of them already, and more are sure to come. I myself have spoken on the issue on numerous occasions (also in *Forum Akademickie*). Today, I could hazard a claim that that wave of criticism did exert some influence on the actions of the parliamentarians (at their request, a list of several dozen publications drawn from the ministerial 'hat' was disclosed) and the ministry itself as it collated a new list of journals. The fundamental change is that the list was not drafted by of a few dozen, or perhaps even several bibliometrists, but was commissioned to forty-four teams, to which about 400 experts were appointed. This list has also been criticised, for example by the experts who found fault with the proposed scores, the experts of the Commission for the Evaluation of Science or the minister himself. On the other hand, more numerous and more confident voices may be heard expressing moderate satisfaction with the list (which I would be inclined to share). Perhaps having some experts assessed by other experts, and these by still others, is a solution to curtail the pathological practices referred to, for example, in the *Code of Ethics for Scholars*. Needless to say, this cannot go on forever, and in the end someone has to make binding decisions, a role which often falls to the minister. It is crucial, though, that they rely on competent rather than just subservient experts, whose opinions are taken seriously. It is also important that the list of the experts, their opinions and assessments are transparent. In fact, the latter requirement has been met with the current list of scientific journals, which I consider to be a significant step in the right direction. If I were to offer a suggestion, I would say that the next step should be to analyse the accuracy of expert evaluations relative to the assessed journals. This could contribute interesting insights to the debate on the correlation between one's viewpoint and one's position. In any case, there is still work to be done to ensure that the terms 'expert' and 'expert opinion' are not treated as an insult to academic decency, and that those who undertake such tasks do not confuse their personal or narrow-group interests with the broader needs of the academic community.

Academic habits

Although habits are determined by innate predispositions, they develop and consolidate as a result of being in a specific external environment. The longer one functions in it, the deeper root they take, only to become routine behaviour in the end. The problem is that some of them make life easier, while others bring about the opposite result. This is also the case with academic habits.

Habits which make life easier

I will mention a few such habits thanks to which the life of at least some academics has become less difficult. Some of them have even gone down in history, such as the custom of punctuality which characterised German philosopher, Immanuel Kant, a professor at the University of Königsberg (now Kaliningrad). In *Kant*, Tadeusz Kroński writes about the scholar's 'proverbial punctuality (the inhabitants of Königsberg reportedly adjusted their clocks to the time the professor always left for his traditional walk …' He adds that 'he knew how to carve out a few hours from his day – divided between work and rest – which he spent carefree with friends'. In Poznań, such a legendary figure was medievalist Kazimierz Tymieniecki, the initiator (in 1919) of the Department of Medieval History at the newly founded University of Poznań. He made history not only due to his seminal works (such as *Początki Państwa Polskiego* [*The Beginnings of the Polish State*]), but also because he regularly went to the university library and spent a lot of time there, even after he retired in 1960. Unfortunately, I did not have the opportunity to meet him on the street, as he died a tragic death – walking lost in thought, he was run over by a tram. Perhaps his habit inspired a joke that was told at the time about a scientist who was asked whether he preferred his wife or his mistress, to which he is said to have replied: 'I would like to have both, because my wife thinks I am at my mistress's, and my mistress thinks I am at my wife's. Meanwhile, I go to the library'. During my time at the AMU, I met a professor of physics who would always take a cab (he did not have a driving licence) to drive him to his institute, located at the other end of Poznań. The professor had considerable achievements in the discipline and was even honoured with a membership of the Polish Academy of Sciences. His immediate family was not thrilled with his ways, as the scholar did not devote much time to them. In the end, they had to get used to it, as did his academic environment. I used to meet another physics professor during my morning walks. He is also a retired scholar now. Nevertheless, he 'hikes' every day (except on public holidays) from his home to his former institute on the outskirts of the city, just like in the 'good old days'. I also met other such 'hiking' retired professors on the campus of my former faculty. It is not unlikely that they were even happy to have found someone who had some time to talk to them. In any case, it is certainly a way to fill up the free time that one has in abundance in retirement.

Keeping up with the latest developments in one's field will also qualify as a habit that facilitates academic life. Nowadays, this is much easier as open access research is often available online, while younger generation of academics have largely honed their skills of using the internet to perfection. Incidentally, I have a colleague who not only relies on this source of information as a matter of principle but also helps me by sending me publications that I would not be able to find. Today, however, internet dependence is exacerbated to a civilisation disease that affects the entire world. When I was in Beijing, I saw for myself that it had even infected a country that had been closed to foreigners for many years. Simultaneously, as I attended various university meetings I realised that there are scholars who find it difficult to live without being 'glued' to their smartphones, even those in high university positions. To an even greater degree, the same is seen among students, now referred to as Generation Z. The generation in question are online even during lectures. I had a student during one of my lectures who was constantly looking at something on his smartphone only to remark at one point that

Wikipedia said something different than what I was saying. Still, following the 'copy and paste' principle when preparing final course papers is a more serious problem, whereas relying on Artificial Intelligence (AI) to write them from start to finish is possibly the gravest. Until recently, one of the most common means of teaching how to think correctly and express oneself in writing was to have students write an essay on a particular topic. Today, this no longer makes much sense, because AI can write it for them not only much faster, but also much better. I do not see any way to wean students off, though the problem is broader than student education at universities. In the article entitled *Artificial Intelligence (AI) in Modifications Business and Passing Unnoticed from Information to Surveillance*, Zdzisław W. Puślecki discusses its business aspects and the significance of AI-powered tools such as ChatGPT in science and education. 'Its advantage is that it is capable of processing vast amounts of data in a very short time; based on that, it can answer questions and solve problems that users prompt it to solve'. The European Commission (the executive body of the European Union) recommends its use for lifelong learning and 'education and training as part of the Erasmus+, European Solidarity Corps and eTwinning programmes'.

Habits which make life difficult

The list of these habits is perhaps even longer than the previous, and certainly more diverse. Personally, I would put sleeping habits at the top. Some people need much more sleep than it would follow from the statistics, but by doing so they lose hours that could otherwise be allocated to effective research work. Another problem is that when they are forced to cut down on sleep due to academic duties, they are sleep-deprived and work less effectively than they would have after a good night's sleep. Furthermore, their competitors in the pursuit of academic success not only sleep less but also think about possible solutions to their research problems while the others are still half awake. The most serious drawback is that the hours of sleep of both groups do not coincide, which reduces the chances of their scientific cooperation. This is by no means a rule, though. I know scientists who had a natural need for long sleep and yet achieved better results than others. Similarly, there is no rule which would universally apply to people who sleep little and do not wake up with but before the roosters. It needs to be noted that fixed working hours for scientists are stipulated in the regulations only at some universities or even selected faculties, while the higher one stands in the academic hierarchy, the more freedom they have to decide when they should work. However, I do not believe that the saying 'sleep tight and the success will come on its own' is the best recommendation for persons who want to make it in the academia.

The habit of taking the floor at every opportunity also ranks high on the list, in my opinion. While it is true that some small children are 'natural born talkers', a scholar is not a child whose guardians let them talk, happy that they can say so much. If such a talker later joins the ranks of scholars, we are likely to end up with a fully-fledged academic prattler. They can be a nuisance to their immediate and extended environment. If they are still a scholar in the making, their environment has the right to expect them to learn something specific first, and only then to speak and, possibly, teach others. On the other hand, if they are scholars with a substantial output, it is not that everyone has to listen to what they have already achieved, or at least could have achieved if others had not interfered. At an advanced age, this proclivity to talk may become – and in many cases does become – a kind of addiction. At various scientific meetings, I often had to deal with the elderly professors who impatiently waited for their turn to speak, and once they were given the floor, they did not know when to stop. They would not respond to the moderators who tried to indicate that their time was over (after all, it is not polite to tell a professor that they have gone off-topic). Naturally, one can also formulate one's views in writing. I am the editor-in-chief of two academic journals and have to say that both the quality and, equally importantly, the volume of submissions is quite a problem. 'Curiously' enough, the word limits adopted in these journals are significantly exceeded by professors of the older generation. With some of them, recommending that they shorten their texts is not a viable option. However, I can ask for the texts to be split into at least two smaller parts (which I sometimes do), and even then, they are quite voluminous.

Treating the duty to conduct classes as if it were the proverbial 'scourge' is another habit that makes life difficult for researchers and students alike. I once had an assistant lecturer who managed to teach only one philosophy class in an entire semester but met the students several times in an establishment (he was partial to alcohol). Ultimately, the students complained about him to the rector, who – after talking to me – decided to terminate his employment. The students today are even more inclined to complain about their academic teachers, which may have actually improved their attendance and regularity of conducting classes. All the same, I do not think that it has radically changed their approach to preparing for classes and adherence to the so-called core curriculum, as this would require plenty of time and effort. And who will compensate them fairly for the effort or at least take it into account in the event of promotions? For a proportion of academics, teaching is their main or even sole responsibility, but they are employed in lower-paid and less appreciated positions. The 2019 law, known as the Act 2.0, has introduced certain safeguards for persons with doctorates employed as lecturers and senior lecturers, but those hoping to rise through the university hierarchy care little about that.

The quirks of scholars

Even outstanding scholars have habits that neither appear to make academic life easier nor more difficult. However, they may readily qualify as strange, sometimes even bizarre. The aforementioned Kant is rightly considered a philosophical exemplar of the European Enlightenment. However, his personal-purpose philosophy was that his rooms in the household should not be aired, since he was convinced that fresh air could harm his poor health. He was fond of tea, but it had to be made using one leaf, as more could be detrimental to his health too, apparently. Although Charles Darwin astonished his scientific contemporaries with his theory of evolution, a number of scientists challenged it, and the scholar avoided direct confrontation with his opponents as much as possible. Describing the famous debate concerning the theory, held on 30 June 1860 at the British Association for the Advancement of Science, M. White and J. Gribbin write that he sent T. Huxley into the battle, 'while [he] pottered around Down House'. The world science would again be amazed by A. Einstein's special and general theory of relativity, but the so-called curious may wonder that he would always sport a 'fresh out of the shower' hairdo that was never combed or that he did not seem concerned about personal hygiene (I have heard such an opinion). Nowadays, the hairstyle may be seen with some politicians (such as the former British Prime Minister Boris Johnson), as well as those who look like the next incarnation of Einstein but lack the same achievement. It may also be surprising to see scholars who keep their hands in their pockets during their lectures (this is relatively common among American professors). One might wonder what they are looking for or even ask whether it is a sign of arrogance. In my academic youth, I heard of a professor who would write accusatory letters against himself signed ‘Sincerely, Anonymous’ and later laughed at the commotion they had caused. It is unlikely that his closest milieu found that just as funny. In comparison, speaking *ex cathedra* as if the fate of the whole world depended on it is a trifle. I have a professor friend who speaks like a ‘prophet’ on official occasions but talks and behaves quite normally in private conversations. However, I will not mention his name because he might take offence.

Academic seriousness

Not infrequently, we happen to be told that what we are saying or doing is silly, or at least asked whether we are being serious. The question becomes particularly important when seriousness is associated with reason, responsibility and propriety of conduct. This is the case, or at least should be the case, in the academic environment. Here, too, seriousness can and often does manifest in quite distinct forms.

Seriousness of the professor

Of all people, a professor definitely has to be a serious person. At least, this is what people who are unfamiliar with the academic life might think. Obviously, I do not mean that a professor is a frivolous person by default. However, I would claim that their seriousness varies in practice. Even when they try to uphold their professorial dignity, the manner of doing so varies. Much depends on their personality and the circumstances in which they live and interact with other academics. I will cite just three examples here. The first is the medieval philosopher and theologian Peter Abelard. In *Intellectuals in the Middle Ages*, Jacques Le Goff states he was 'the glory of the Parisian milieu', 'the first great modern intellectual figure – within the limits of the term "modernity" in the twelfth century. (...) the first *professor*'. Among his character traits, Le Goff mentions 'the need to destroy idols' and such 'self-confidence' that 'led him to attack the most illustrious of the Parisian masters, William of Champeaux'. In a letter to a friend, Abelard wrote that he 'approached the old man who owed his reputation more to his advanced age than to his talent or his culture. (...) He was admirable in the eyes of his hearers, but of no account in the sight of questioners'. Such opinions earned him the recognition of some and backlash from others. One of his most vocal and influential opponents was Bernard of Clairvaux. In the *Letter to Magister Ivo, Cardinal of the Roman Curia*, he wrote that 'Master Peter Abelard, monk without a rule, prelate without responsibility, neither holds an order nor is held by an order. He is a man unlike himself: a Herod within, a John without; double through and through, having nothing of a monk about him except the name and the habit'. This negative opinion may have been provoked not only by Abelard's philosophical views (since he supported nominalism and conceptualism, condemned by the Church), but also due to his affair with his student Heloise (such relationships between teacher and student are still prohibited and socially censured). Although the affair adds a significant element to his personality as a man, it takes something away from his professorial seriousness. Philosophers, however, consider Abelard to be a serious professor who contributed to the revival of Aristotle's authority, while psychologists see him as a pioneer in removing the stigma of 'diabolic possession' from mental illness ('he disproved the notion that the devil caused madness').

In the modern era, Isaac Newton was an outstanding professor, and to some extent he still is. During his academic life, he was depicted in several paintings, whose reproductions may be found in Frank E. Manuel's biography of the scientist, *A Portrait of Isaac Newton*. It appears that he became more and more serious as time went by, and the 1729 painting shows not only a serious but also a haughty mien. This is somewhat understandable. Although he climbed the academic ladder quite quickly at Trinity College, Cambridge (having obtained his master's degree at the age of just 27), his greatest academic achievements (such as formulating the principles of classical mechanics) came a little later – his seminal *Mathematical Principles of Natural Philosophy*, was first published in 1687. He came to head the Royal Society even later; although he was inducted as a member of that English academy of sciences at a fairly early age (in 1672), he only took over as the chair in 1703 (following the death of one of his chief scientific adversaries, Robert Hooke). The aforementioned biographer entitled that particular chapter in Newton's academic life *The Autocrat of Science*. Even so, he admits that on the continent his magnum opus 'aroused as much doubt as it did admiration in England'. Newton was aware that it was not perfect and introduced revisions in the subsequent editions. This demonstrates that he approached both his own views as well as the grave reservations voiced with respect to his work with professorial seriousness. Much can be said about that scholar, but not that he was inclined to jokes, or even to accept the casual lifestyle of his friend, poet and reveller Lord Montagu Ch. Halifax – likewise a member of the Royal Society and Newton's protector. Manuel states that Newton 'burned all of Halifax's letters but one, which he kept as an admirable example of unfulfilled court promises and professions' (concerning a significant part of estate to be bequeathed to Newton in the reveller's will).

Was the contemporary physicist Albert Einstein prone to jokes? A photo of the scientist with his tongue sticking out is widely known to media consumers, but the scientist could only afford to clown in this fashion when he had already achieved his greatest scientific successes, recognised with the 1921 Nobel Prize for 'his contribution to theoretical physics, particularly for his discovery of the law of the photoelectric effect'. Roger Highfield and Paul Carter analysed *The Private Lives of Albert Einstein* and the picture they painted shows that he was not a joker. On the contrary, he took both his private and academic life very seriously. During the period of his life which saw him gain worldwide fame and respect, even among those who 'only the haziest understanding of his discoveries', he publicly spoke out on many important social issues. His collection of writings, entitled *How I See The World*, included the *Message to Intellectuals*, which was to be delivered at the World Congress of Intellectuals in Defence of Peace, held in Wrocław in August 1948. The censors at the time found it too anti-communist to be presented at the meeting. This of course reflects badly on the censors rather than scholar, because a professor of his calibre has the right, even a duty to speak out on serious issues such as world peace; plus, and in democratic countries, his voice is taken into account by the political authority.

The so-called deadly seriousness

Although this heading derives from colloquial language, it can still apply to academic life. It may connote a funeral ceremony – because where else but during a burial are the participants expected at least to express their feelings with due solemnity, if they are not capable of showing earnest sympathy to the family and loved ones of the deceased. This also applies to the obsequies of members of the academic community. The more eminent the deceased, the more people usually take part in the ceremony and the more people feel obliged to express their grief and sympathy. This does not require a full farewell address, but certainly deserves a few words said to the deceased's loved ones or, failing that, a mournful countenance. In the case of university's important figures, the funeral at the cemetery is preceded by a valediction at the university, with the individual's closest associates standing guard by their coffin or urn – with a serious expression on their faces, of course. If the rector attends the event, they are usually responsible for delivering the farewell tribute. However, they may delegate this task to one of the deputies, which actually often happens. In that case, that person merely reads the letter from their superior, which may still appear serious but much of that seriousness is lost when the letter only repeats the words that are already in the official university obituary. Things become even less solemn when the person assigned to perform this task does so in such a hurry as if they were racing against the clock to attend another ceremony. The sense of seriousness diminishes even further when people come to the ceremony just to gawk or meet someone they know and exchange critical remarks about the deceased.

Often enough, the situations in which the 'be or not to be' of members of the academic community is decided involves so-called deadly seriousness as well. For many years, postdoctoral defences were just such occasions. I took part in many as a member of the faculty council authorised to award this academic degree, and as a reviewer in such a procedure. There were situations where some members of the panel failed to take their duties seriously and did not even try to hide it (by not participating in the meeting), although this was not the case with the postdoctoral candidates. As regards the latter, if they displayed certain self-confidence, they would do so with a serious demeanour, intended to convince those who decided on the academic promotion that they deserve it. However, much of that confidence would fade when the reviewers voiced major reservations about their scientific achievement or asked questions that they were unable to answer meaningfully. At times, however, the questions did not actually match the scope of their research interests. Still, the members who were the real terror on this panel considered it their duty to ask questions – with an air of 'deadly' seriousness – that were apparently designed to test the competence of the candidate but instead showed that the asker did not understand what that candidate did. The battle for an academic's 'to be or not to be' also took place during doctoral programme interviews, which I experienced from both sides: as a candidate and a member of the admissions committee. In the former case, I faced a panel member who did not take what I said very seriously and decided to admit a person who later failed to write their dissertation. Fortunately for me, another person on that committee found me qualified enough – not so much for the doctoral programme as to work as a researcher and teacher at the AMU Institute of Philosophy, where I was hired as an assistant lecturer (and defended my doctoral thesis three years later). Once an independent researcher, I would sit for many years on the admissions committee for doctoral studies in philosophy. The members of that body approached their duty of selecting the best candidates with varying degrees of seriousness. Certain persons there would only become more active when a student whose master's they had supervised applied. Often enough, they maintained with deadly seriousness that those candidates had an exceptional talent for research work. In a proportion of cases, it would turn out to be true, whereas sometimes the alleged 'genius' had considerable problems with submitting a doctoral dissertation of adequate quality and in a timely manner. All I want to say is that the deadly seriousness of the opinion-givers may sometimes help people of average ability to achieve some success in academic life, but it cannot make up for their lack of scientific aptitude and the diligence that is prerequisite for such success.

The seriousness of the rector

Found in the office of the rector at my former university (AMU), the gallery of portraits of all the rectors since the university was founded is a reason enough to add a word or two about the seriousness which that position involves. The persons commemorated in those paintings manifest their gravitas not only in their countenances, but also through the insignia of rectorial authority, such as robes and chains. I had my dealings with many of them, first as a student and then, for several decades, as a researcher and teacher at this university. I do not want to go into too much detail, but I will say that some among the former rectors earned my considerable respect, whereas others did not deserve the same kind of recognition, or at any rate did nothing I would find memorable, apart perhaps from the fact that some of them cared more about good relations with the political surroundings than about academic values and greatnesses. Were many like that? This I cannot answer because it is not proper to speak ill of the dead. Still, it would be appropriate to mention one former rector, who was not just portrayed as a serious figure, but also took his official duties so seriously that he antagonised the university's light-hearted and malcontent while gaining recognition from those who treated their duties seriously as well. I also have fond memories of a former rector who may look (no offence meant) a little self-conscious in his gown and chain in the picture, but who otherwise – at less official and private gatherings – demonstrated such a musical talent and ease as if music were his natural element. That won him recognition of some and earned disfavour among those who believed that such music-making did not befit a rector and professor with a substantial scientific achievement.

Academic jokes

For a joke to be a joke, it must not only be tailored to the sense of humour of those who tell it, but also to their audience. After all, what amuses some may not necessarily amuse many others, or even happen to be incomprehensible. The academics who have addressed their jokes to persons outside their milieu have repeatedly found out that this is precisely the case.

The so-called crude jokes

The division into 'crude' and 'subtle' jokes is not universal, but it has been used for quite some time. Of course, the yardsticks of their 'crudeness' and 'subtlety' can and do differ. Let me draw here on the tradition of philosophers poking fun at one another and those around them. According to *The Lives of the Eminent Philosophers* by Diogenes Laertius, one of the most colourful figures of ancient times was Socrates. His demeanour was admired by some, while others saw it as an opportunity for crude jokes, such as those found in Aristophanes' comedy *The Clouds*. Socrates is portrayed there as a person who 'haughtily strides the streets of Athens' while dressed in rags unbefitting a decent citizen. Laertius also mentions the philosopher's sense of humour: 'When Xanthippe first scolded him and then drenched him with water, his rejoinder was, "Did I not say that Xanthippe's thunder would end in rain?"' Some people sympathised with Socrates, but a few actually sided with his argumentative wife, such as the German philosopher F. Nietzsche, who thought Xanthippe's indignation was utterly justified. After all, instead of practicing his learned craft of a stonemason, Socrates roamed the streets of

Athens and importuned the young by questioning the belief in many gods and their agency. One can really wonder whether this is said in jest or seriously; if it is a joke indeed, then it is quite a crude one.

At a time when philosophy became a 'servant' of theology, philosophers made no jokes about the latter, and if they did, they did so cautiously so as not to fall foul of the church censors. This began to change in the late fifteenth and the early sixteenth century, as evinced, for example, by Erasmus of Rotterdam's *In Praise of Folly*. The very title is already a sarcastic joke, mocking the then academics as well as all those who 'trumpeted' their own glory, while being the living embodiment of foolishness. That group comprised the Stoics (who consider themselves 'almost equal to the gods') and the Pythagoreans (who invented some mysterious 'quaternion' which supposedly explains the source of all life). There is also no shortage of physicians ('in this profession, those that have most confidence, though the least skill, shall be sure of the greatest custom'), 'fraudster lawyers' and 'ridicule-worthy astrologers'. The list is far from complete but, based on it, it is unlike to elicit laughter in people whom Erasmus of Rotterdam met, for instance when giving lectures at the universities of Louvain and Oxford. However, his work met with considerable recognition among the libertines (freethinkers). In *French Free-Thought from Gassendi to Voltaire*, J. S. Spink notes that 'what made the academic libertine was the fact that he was a scholar, an erudite, with a full share of *libido sciendi* [lust for knowledge]'. How did this manifest? An answer is supplied by the Jesuit F. Garasse, who was outraged by his jokes. He speaks of the libertine: 'as for ceremonies and ecclesiastical traditions, visions, apparitions and such like, he will call them in mockery the offal of religion. (...) to give a ridiculous turn to an idea he will invent a saying full of scorn and profanation of sacred things, as for example to describe somebody's zigzag gait he will say that he walks like a dog just come from vespers'.

In the nineteenth century, the theory of evolution by Charles Darwin was deemed a sacrilege in ecclesiastical circles. Darwin was not an academic warrior, ready to openly confront the supporters of divine creationism. His student Thomas Huxley, also known as 'Darwin's bulldog', was happy to do it for him. In their biography of Darwin, M. White and J. Gribbin recount the confrontation between supporters and opponents of the theory of evolution, which took place in Oxford on 30 June 1860, during the 'fateful meeting of the British Association for the Advancement of Science'. The opponents were represented by Samuel Wilberforce, the Bishop of Oxford, while Huxley's spoke for the proponents. The former asked the latter: 'Is it on his grandfather's or his grandmother's side that the ape ancestry comes in?' In response, he heard: 'I should feel it no shame to have risen from such an origin. But I should feel it a shame to have sprung from one who prostituted the gifts of culture and of eloquence to the service of prejudice and of falsehood'. Naturally, one could argue whether these are crude jokes or even whether they are jokes at all. According to the above biographers, 'Wilberforce was joking and trying to defuse a potentially nasty scene'. Even if that had been the case, the news of the meeting 'spread far and wide within the intellectual community', while Darwin and his supporters were 'riding the crest of an ideological wave'.

The so-called subtle jokes

Although this category of jokes is just as vague as the previous, one can cite examples of such jokes that fall within the latter rather than the former category. In this case, too, one can refer to Socrates. According to the German philosopher Georg W. F. Hegel, the essence of Socrates' method of seeking the truth was irony, conveyed most succinctly in his 'I know that I know nothing'. 'What he wished to effect was, that when other people brought forward their principles, he, from each definite proposition, should deduce as its consequence the direct opposite of what the proposition stated, or else allow the opposite to be deduced from their own inner consciousness without maintaining it directly against their statements'. If anyone finds this explanation convoluted, they should ask those who have taken the trouble to familiarise themselves with any major treatise of the German philosopher (according to K. R. Popper, he was a 'master' of tortuous disquisition). However, it looks much more straightforward in the philosophical dialogues attributed to Socrates (but written by his closest disciple, Plato). In each, prior to questions being asked of Socrates, one outlines the circumstances which offer a rationale behind them. The role of master and teacher falls to Socrates, whereas those willing to listen to his questions and attempt to answer become the students. Socrates may mock the ineptitude of some, but he does not leave them without his intellectual support. As for those who believe themselves to be superior to Socrates as teachers, are unceremoniously confronted with the power of his arguments. This group includes, for example, Protagoras and Gorgias, Sophists known from the titles of his dialogues. If the joke is to 'have their backs to the wall' so that 'they can no longer say yea or nay', then the joke is quite subtle. For a philosopher like Socrates, however, it was no joke that they turned sophistry into eristic, that is, the art of giving falsehoods the pretence of truth.

Modern times not only saw the spread of printing but also the rise of superior epistolary writing. This is evident, for instance, in the letters that scholars wrote to other scholars or at least to those who were interested in their achievements. Many of such letters offer examples of subtle criticism that perhaps did not require their addressees to be willing to alter their views but at least demanded a degree of discernment which would enable them to tell jest from communication in earnest. One of such epistles, *To these Wisest and Most Distinguished Men, the Dean and Doctors of the Holy Faculty of Theology at the University of Paris*, was written by R. Descartes as a kind of appendix to his *Meditations on First Philosophy*. It matters little that they are the 'Wisest and Most Distinguished' and the 'name of the Sorbonne has such authority', if they should learn something from his work, provided that 'deign to take an interest' in it. It turned out that the learned men did and formulated their *First Objections*. It clearly follows from Descartes' replies that they either failed to understand his work or even misunderstood it altogether, for instance where it concerns the impotence of God and the power of the human mind (the meditating 'ego cogito'). Obviously, Descartes' thought was not without major weaknesses, which the authors of the other six *Objections of the Learned Men* pointed out. Descartes did not find any to be valid and, in the *Letter to Father Dinet*, he stated that he was 'astounded to realise that I would have to revise my view completely (...). In the brief set of *Meditations* which [he] published are to be found all the principles of the philosophy on which I am working'.

This approach would prompt many later philosophers not only to question the rationality of Cartesianism, but also of any philosophy that aspires to be objective truth. One of them was American philosopher Richard McKay Rorty (professor at Princeton and Stanford). In the book entitled *Contingency, Irony, and Solidarity*, he described himself as an ironist for whom nothing is sacred. However, such an ironist has one major concern, namely that 'someday my remote descendants will live in a global civilisation in which love is pretty much the only law'. All other 'universal' claims and expectations should be completely abandoned. In his *Intellectual Autobiography*, he wrote that after the publication of *Contingency…* he 'grew accustomed to being asked whether I still consider myself a philosopher. My reply was: "Sure. What else can I call myself? I have read too little outside of philosophy to qualify as a member of any other discipline." When asked whether I am still an analytic philosopher, I reply "Only on Tuesdays and Thursdays" – the point being that I work on both of the tracks I distinguished earlier'. As to whether 'analytic philosophy will "win" (…) or will wither away', Rorty replied: 'I have no idea which will happen, but I do not think that the question is of much importance'. Such subtle jokes did not appeal to the American analytical philosophers who enjoyed considerable acclaim at academic centres such as the University of Virginia (where Rorty was a professor of humanities in 1982–1998). In his *Autobiography*, Rorty mentions that his *Contingency…* met with 'devastatingly bad reviews' from them.

Interesting ironists may also be found in our Polish 'backyard', such as philosopher and theologian (lecturer at the Pontifical Academy of Theology in Krakow) Józef Tischner. He would often sign his numerous publications using pseudonyms such as Wawrzek Chowaniec, Molinista, Józek Szkolny, or Jegomość Józek. Each moniker contains an element of self-irony, stemming – among other things – from the fact that a boy from Łopuszna (a village in the Nowy Targ district) not only became an academic professor, but also a close friend of Pope John Paul II. His theory of truth: 'There's three truths: holy truth, truth too, and shit truth [bullshit]' gained quite some notoriety. However you look at it, that joke is fairly crude, but much more subtle ones are contained in his book entitled *Historia filozofii po góralsku* [*History of Philosophy the Highlander Way*]. Using the dialect of the Tatra mountains, the author discusses the 'Highlander' view of that history. And so, 'in the beginning, there were highlanders, and only later did Turks and Jews appear. (…) In books, the first wise man is called Tales, but his real name was Stasek Nedza, not from Miletus, but from Parddałówka. His father herded sheep and traded horses'. Here, the crudeness or subtlety of the joke can hardly be determined conclusively. There is no doubt, however, that such jokes have invariably amused people who can exercise some perspective towards philosophy and themselves as well. The reception of said jokes also varied. In *Ksiądz na manowcach* [*A Priest Astray*], Tischner mentions that he once 'indulged in a joke about himself. When asked whether he felt more a priest or a philosopher, he replied: "First, I feel like a human, then a philosopher, and only then a priest." That statement sparked protests. People would say: "It's unbecoming."'

Naturally, it is not just philosophers who are capable of jokes. If I refer primarily to philosophers, it is because I am relatively familiar with philosophical traditions and at least believe myself able to comprehend the meaning of some of their jokes. I do not insist that philosophy is, or at least may be the same science as many other sciences. What I do assert is that certain forms used by philosophers to ridicule their fellow thinkers and philosophy as such enabled them to maintain a distance not only towards the views held by others, but also towards their own. However, there is always the danger that a philosophy which employs humour can itself become a poor joke. Hence it follows that even when joking, moderation is highly advised.

Academic courage

In many situations in life, courage is a prerequisite of success, but it is also indispensable in order to survive the most serious threats, keep one's holdings or at least incur the least possible losses. The problem is that courage must not only be mustered but also adapted to the circumstances. Academic courage is no exception here.

The 'mindless' courage

The 'headless horseman' is such a universal literary metaphor that it may also apply to academic life. The 'rider' may be both a novice in the academic profession and someone who has practiced it for a relatively long time but has not yet mastered the art of climbing the academic promotion ladder to the extent that they are stuck 'treading water' – which is still tolerable – or, worse yet, have to look for another job. In the case of people writing a doctoral dissertation, such may be the fallout of the authors' questioning the scientific qualifications of their supervisor and potential reviewers or failure to include their achievements in the references. There are supervisors and reviewers who are not particularly sensitive about their scientific merit, but they are relatively few. On the other hand, those who start the assessment of a doctoral dissertation by checking how they are represented there are quite numerous. For some, even criticism voiced by doctoral students in less official circumstances may be a cause of distress. I know of a supervisor who was advised by an obliging yet anonymous individual that his doctoral student spoke disparagingly of him in private conversations. He nursed the grudge so well that he would later tenaciously go against the former student, even when he was already a full professor and had made both an academic and a political career. Although formally no supervisors are involved when applying for a postdoctoral degree, the reviewers and members of postdoctoral committees can cause the candidate a lot of grief. One such aspiring postdoc I know dared to omit the scientific achievements of a member of his postdoctoral panel in the submitted dissertation. He was greatly fortunate because it was a person appointed to sit on the committee and their vote was not the majority vote. They were so offended by the fact as to announce that they would appear at the meeting where the relevant discipline council decided the award of the degree, to persuade that body to go with their negative opinion. Ultimately, however, they had no desire to travel halfway across Poland or take part in that meeting remotely.

One could, of course, ask about the courage it takes to tackle serious problems and put forward bold hypotheses. According to Karl R. Popper, they contribute the most to progress in science, though on the necessary condition that the hypotheses are resolvable and that attempts are made to eliminate the most fallacious ones. That kind of courage is seen in various sciences, but more often in some and less often in others. The fact that the proportion of courageous scientists in the exact and natural sciences is higher than in the social sciences and humanities is not much of an issue; the real problem is that it is easier to expose oneself to ridicule with dubious hypotheses in the latter. This applies in equal measure to novice scientists and persons with considerable scientific expertise, even those who have gained acclaim in the academic community. Sigmund Freud is an eloquent example. The Austrian psychologist is considered the 'founding father' of analytical psychology, whose essential principles he expounded in *The Psychopathology of Everyday Life*, published in 1901. According to that theory, the human psyche consists of the id, the ego and the superego, but there is also libido, a sexualised energy source underlying erotic relations and emotions (such as love, hate and guilt). Until his death, Freud maintained that 'psychoanalysis is part of the psychological science of the mind' and that it 'has a special right to defend the scientific worldview'. Meanwhile, in *The Foundations of Psychoanalysis*, Adolf Grünbaum, describes psychoanalysis as an 'exegetical myth of "scientific self-misunderstanding"', while its cornerstone, Freudian clinical theory, is 'philosophical speculation parasitising on science'. Another critical assessment of the theory comes from the Australian psychologist Malcolm Macmillan, who states in *Freud Evaluated* that 'Freud's method is neither capable of yielding objective data about mental processes nor of potential value for those seeking to turn psychoanalysis into an acceptable historical or humanistic discipline'. Obviously, there are also psychologists who not only recognise its scientific value, but also employ it in their clinical practice. Either way, Freud is Freud, and it may be worthwhile to at least seriously analyse the pros and cons of the premises he adopted and the hypotheses formulated on those grounds. Still, quite a few 'headless horsemen' have the courage to call themselves clinical psychologists and charge money from people willing to use their services, but when the push comes to shove, no 'specialist' will help you if do not do it yourself. Some time ago, Poland saw a well-publicised case of a sexologist from Poznań who was eventually brought to court and convicted of sexual abuse. I should add that this person had the courage to work as a professional sexologist, even though he had obtained his postdoctoral degree in pedagogy.

The 'mindful' courage

Although virtually everyone is born with a head, few are natively possessed of the wits to protect themselves from threats to their lives and their functioning in a particular environment. As a rule, they need the help of their parents and carers to acquire such skills. In academic life, this role belongs, among others, to the supervisors of master's theses and doctoral dissertations. However, one has to successfully choose those who, first of all, are willing to take care of us and, second, are able to help rather than do harm. In the latter case, overprotective supervisors who notice that their students are overwhelmed by the task, tend to solve research problems for them and generously allow their students to submit the work under their own name. However, there are also supervisors who have high expectations of themselves and their charges alike, and if the student fails to meet them, they have to look for another supervisor. Sometimes they do find one, though they have to be careful not to get out of the proverbial frying pan into the fire. At any rate, they have to keep their head on straight while doing so. Of course, this bit of 'headwork' does not end with the preparation and defence of a doctoral dissertation. It is even more difficult at the postdoctoral level, where has to take more numerous and diverse reviewers into account. Still, where there is a will, there is a way to pass this threshold in one's academic career. I once acted as a reviewer in a postdoctoral qualification procedure in which the submitted thesis was not particularly impressive, but the candidate had so much 'backing' among the professors, that the qualification panel found her scientific achievement outstanding enough to be entered for the rector's award. It certainly cannot be said that that postdoctoral candidate was a 'headless horseman'.

The 'headwork' it takes earn professorship can almost be considered an art form. Meeting the statutory requirements to obtain the title is less of an issue, since they are so general that they can be interpreted and 'bent' to the needs and possibilities of professorial candidates. The chief problem is that the reviewers also interpret those provisions in their own fashion and construe such requirements as 'significant contribution to a given discipline or field' or international scientific cooperation literally. Consequently, they will not 'turn a blind eye' to the fact that the purported achievement is at best an overview of the achievements of other scientists, while the international collaboration is no more than a sightseeing tour of foreign academic centres. I say this as someone who has repeatedly been a reviewer in professorial procedures and has often determined that the candidate did not meet the statutory requirements. I suppose that more than one has racked their brains to figure out how to avoid ending up with me on the panel. This was already difficult with the previous mode of selecting expert reviewers, because the criterion of competence did play a role in their appointment. It seems even more difficult now, as the opinion panel is more numerous (previously at least four persons, now there must be at least five), while none of them may represent the same academic institution as the candidate; in addition, they are drawn from a group of fifteen reviewers.

If so, what can be done to overcome these difficulties? My answer is simple: one's achievement has to be so substantial that even the most demanding reviewers will find it difficult to challenge. Of course, this is easier said than done, as evinced by the relatively advanced age of those who are awarded the title of professor. Medical and health sciences are the exception, though I am not saying that they are particularly abundant in scientific talent. However, the methods that appear to have developed within those sciences – enabling one to overcome obstacles on the path to professorship relatively quickly – are not that widespread in other disciplines. Naturally, I do not mean to offend medical scholars, but I need to note that a close friend of mine – a professor at a medical university – claims that it is unthinkable for one to be promoted there if they omit their superiors in their publications. I did hear about such practices at my former university (AMU), but they were rather rare. I will not mention the one instance I know about, as it is better to say nothing about the deceased than to speak ill of them.

There are, of course, many other ways to win the favour of those who decide on academic promotions. Traditional methods include quoting – regardless of whether it is substantively justified (hence publications that are often 'swollen' with citations). Another proven method is to compliment the potential reviewers at various scientific encounters. Those who have the right 'clout' at their university may also try to have them recognised with an honorary award (preferably an honorary doctorate). On the other hand, those who only have the necessary financial means may organise a meeting (under the label of a scientific conference), where such persons will experience choice hospitality catering-wise. Meanwhile, those with an extensive social network may reach them through other, friendly contacts. I will certainly not claim that all these methods are resorted to in every case. I would argue, however, that in an academic environment it is best to be born a professor, and if that is not possible, it is best to start intensive research work at a relatively young age and persevere doing so until retirement or even longer.

When asked if they are not afraid of prosecution, politicians sometimes claim that they are only afraid of God and their wives. Although more inquisitive investigative journalists could sometimes show that even such words are unfounded, because they may be at peace with God, but they are on the 'warpath' with their wives. However, there is something courageous in making such declarations (especially when it concerns politicians from the so-called back benches). Can the same be said about academics? I do not think so. Firstly, because a large proportion do not really believe in divine justice and, secondly, because an even greater number would like justice served 'here and now' – provided, of course, that it is on their side. Is any political authority able to meet these expectations? It is probably easier for those who understand the needs of the academic community well. However, I would advise waiting a while to answer the question the current political authority fits the bill, because for now only some of its promises have been put into practice, while the list is quite long. One can also seriously ponder if the rectors who received their mandate in the 2024 elections will meet the expectations of the university community by. Although not even a year has passed since the elections, we can already say that some of them are coping better with the problems of their universities, while others are doing worse – as evidenced by, among other things, their financial and personnel struggles publicised in the media. However, I would not like to take on the role of those prosecutors who conduct proceedings in cases of financial abuse committed by the authorities of several universities, nor of those journalists who track down plagiarists and, exposing them, they also bring to light the actions of university bodies that fail to keep up with the practices of plagiarists and their defenders. However, these problems are very real and need to be talked about openly.

The zones of shouting and silence

In everyone's life, there are zones where there is room for shouting, and spheres where silence should predominate. Sometimes the former is desired, sometimes one craves the latter. However, next to people's needs, much depends on whether they can be satisfied and understood by others. In the academic environment, tolerance to shouting and silence is required as well.

The zones of shouting

The saying that a person is born screaming is one of those self-evident truisms. However, if anyone is in doubt on that score, they should make the effort to visit a hospital delivery room. I have never been in one myself, but I have heard the accounts of women who gave birth that have reinforced my conviction that it is better to be born a man. Natural noise zones also include playgrounds for small children, especially those adjacent to nursery schools. Even preschoolers can manage a volume that carries their yelling far beyond the playground. The opportunities to express their emotions through shouting are more limited for primary school pupils, though not to the extent that they cannot show off their vocal range during breaks between lessons. The restrictions on shouting in secondary schools are even more stringent. However, the teenagers can go to a stadium and scream with other fans as if they were possessed. Just a small joke there.

Still, the point is to at least attempt to determine the origin of the noise in the zones where students live and function, such as student residences. I lived in one throughout my studies and often found that there was no better opportunity to demonstrate the full potential of a student's voice than during Saturday/Sunday stints with friends over a bottle (or more) of beer. Student festivals and picnics organised by universities are a particular opportunity to let the voice go far and wide. In my student days, such events took place both on the campus and in the city streets. Those held in town came to an end after a female student suffered a fatal accident. However, they would still be held at a campus located near a housing estate. The residents repeatedly complained to the university authorities about the students disturbing their night's sleep. And? Well, not much can be done to stop the students from shouting, yelling and screaming.

In many countries, locations which qualify as shouting zones witness various street demonstrations. Not only do students take part, but often also initiate such protests, as was the case during the student spring of 1968, for instance. The largest and most intense were seen in France, sweeping through the entire Latin Quarter in Paris as well as other French cities. In Poland, the disturbances would come to be known as 'March '68', but they were not as massive, nor did they bring about such changes in higher education as in France. The demonstrations following the introduction of martial law in Poland in December 1981 reached a much larger scale. Although the students did not dare to take to the streets against this attempt to stifle the democratic transformation, they did occupy interiors at many Polish universities. This changed after the watershed of 1989, that is, in the so-called independent Poland. It is now easier for students to publicly manifest their needs (whether by shouting or stating their demands on the placards) as well as make demands that are essentially impossible to satisfy; suffice it to mention the call for 'residences for 1 zloty' as an example.

If anyone thinks that students can shout out their needs, but that it does not befit academic professors to do so, they should read the article by Andrzej Białas entitled 'A Cry of Despair', published in *PAUza Akademicka*, no. 715. The author cites the 'texts by well-known legal authorities, professors Andrzej Zoll, Andrzej Mączyński and Jan Widacki, who critically comment on the text in which professor Grzegorz Bartosz (*PAUza Akademicka* no. 703), urged to counter the flood of lies in the public space (mainly online, though not exclusively), also by legal means. The statements of prominent lawyers are unequivocal: the law is not suited for controlling the truthfulness of public information, and its application would cause more harm than good.

It would entail the threat of censorship and restrict freedom of expression, thus violating of one of the essential human rights'. Such 'cries of despair' have also frequently featured on the pages of *Forum Akademickie*, a periodical devoted to all things academic. Many of them are concerned with the method adopted in our country to parametrise scientific facilities. Jerzy Kołodziejczak, professor at the Jagiellonian University, describes the recent attempts to improve it as 'powdering the corpse'. There is reason enough to be loud about it because, under the parameterisation criteria applied in 2020–2023, the list of the 'best' research units now includes institutions that employ few scientists, hardly any of whom is known outside their immediate milieu. On the other hand, the achievement of quite a few such scholars consists primarily of publications purchased with the so-called predatory journals. The assessment of scientific journals gives rise to some uproar as well. It has a number of advocates, of course, because their universities can afford to foot the bill for papers published by the predators. However, a number of universities are too poor for that or, alternatively, the scholars employed there simply believe that their work should stand on its own by virtue of their professional qualifications.

In my academic life, I have also occasionally heard exclamations of joy and such bitterness that it would be difficult to describe it in a nutshell. I would hear the former mainly outside the door of my university office, after a student had successfully passed an exam. The latter, on the other hand, tended to be uttered by candidates for a postdoctoral degree or professorship who received negative opinions and were unable to accept the fact. They were entitled to appeal against the decision of the bodies authorised to award this degree and title, and often filed such appeals, but that was rarely effective. Sometimes, the additional reviewers appointed to evaluate their achievement were even harsher in their assessments. At times joyful cheers accompanied the end of the term of a rector or dean who would make life hard for the individuals who did not appreciate or simply did not like them. Conversely, cries of sadness ensued when such functionaries realised they had exhausted the possibilities of running for another term. In either case, however, such manifestations were fairly discreet. In fact, those who vehemently opposed an unwelcome candidate throughout the entire election process would sometimes rush to congratulate them, feigning joy after their victory.

The zones of silence

For many people, cemeteries are such a zone; one may even choose to describe silence as 'sepulchral' or 'deathly'. Still, science and academic teaching are not dead yet, while the fact that it does not always present a picture of health is a different matter altogether. Bedrooms can also be such a zone, at least where spouses are not 'at each other's throats'. However, there is a lot of truth in Francisco de Goya's piece entitled *The Sleep of Reason Produces Monsters*. With scholars, these 'monsters' may – in their dreams – assume the form of those who have given them a hard time. Some monsters may also remind them of the mistakes they have made or educational shortcomings such as poor command of the language required to perform successfully on an international forum. Either way, one can dream of pleasant and unpleasant things. Once awake, we may be faced with either silence or shouting. The former is more common among scholars who have understanding spouses and well-behaved children. If this is not the case, they can go to a library reading room, where silence is the rule. However, today's academics rarely visit libraries because they usually have a computer at hand with which they can shut themselves away in their room and work until someone becomes concerned about their prolonged absence. Still, all that describes situations where the power and capacity of particular scientists to impose or enter a quiet zone is quite limited.

And yet, there are zones whose ultimate nature is decided by the scholars themselves: the zones where one's failures and one's achievements are talked about. Some prefer to remain utterly silent about their fiascos, because discussing them will gladden the opponents and sadden their friends and supporters. Not everything can be 'cloaked with a veil of silence'. Nearly always someone will be there to remind us of the mistakes and even recount them in a manner that will put us to shame. Others will proclaim their latest achievements – such having a text published by a prestigious journal or publisher – wherever and to whomever they can. I know a professor who does this on a regular basis. Perhaps, if he exercised a little more restraint, he would not lose a little of his professorial dignity on each such occasion. It is believed that one can either speak well of the dead or not at all, even about those who have left the worst impression in our memory. It is even more difficult when the person was well known and caused such damage with their reckless actions that many will long have to bear the consequences.

Such individuals are relatively easy to find in politics and among the academics who confused their academic duties with political tasks. Such individuals have functioned at many public universities, including the Adam Mickiewicz University. I will not mention them by name, not only out of respect for the deceased, but also because hardly anyone needs it today. Still, there is such a thing as reckoning with the past, which did not spare certain late figures who otherwise contributed significantly to the history of science. Numerous publications released after the watershed of 1989 did precisely that, though the assessments and opinions formulated there often diverged quite radically. As for my own conclusion, I would say that such reckonings are necessary, but a better future of the academic life in Poland cannot be built on such a foundation alone.

The tacit and the 'cluckers'

Here, I draw on the once widely known satirical piece written in 1964 by Janusz Szpotański, *The Tacit and the Cluckers, or A Ball at the President's, an Opera in Three Acts with an Overture and Finale*. However, I have no intention of revisiting the times of W. Gomułka, nor to throw such a satirical spotlight on the situation of those who have or at least could have something significant to say in academic life – if only they dared to speak. But either they do not speak, or they speak in a manner that their voice can at best be considered as some kind of 'clucking'. There are various reasons for keeping shush like that or for speaking so as to avoid causing harm – heaven forbid – to oneself. The young academics might fear saying something so inconvenient for their superiors that the latter would easily find an opportunity to have them stripped of their academic position. Naturally, they may suggest something, such as reading a publication that presents a completely different point of view on an issue. However, this is also risky since it would imply that their superiors are not entirely up to date with the developments in the field, or that they have not even bothered to read what they need to stay up to date. Now, if they do not remain silent, they 'cluck' in a way that it is impossible to tell whether they agree or disagree with their superiors' views. It does not befit a scholar with the status of an independent researcher to speak as if they did not know what they are talking about, but it is advisable to at least avoid the most sensitive issues in conversations with persons to whom one owes their academic advancement. However, this is a kind of 'high-skill game' that is sometimes called 'diplomacy', and sometimes simply 'good manners'. Does science suffer as a result? Not necessarily. After all, it is possible to choose a research path that does not conflict with the path of one's superiors. Ultimately, a new job may be found where researchers are of a like mind or at least have a matching level of scientific competence. The latter option is chosen by the relatively most ambitious, but they are not so few as to be considered a 'dying breed'. Obviously, in each case such a migration incurs the risk of encountering someone who is on such good terms with one's former superiors that they will readily cause the 'hiker' some headache – as a friendly favour. Indeed, the profession of a scientist looks like 'plain sailing' only to the less informed, while in fact having someone 'killed' in the line of duty (intellectually, of course) is relatively easy.

Student resourcefulness

The image of the student in public awareness varies, spanning both the 'beggar' student and one who may not all too well off, but nevertheless has heaps of fun living an academic life on credit, courtesy of their parents or the state. Between these extremes, there is a kind of 'grey area' of students who study a little and party a little too, looking forward to the next exam session with some unease. Those are the most numerous.

Resourcefulness in life

I could say a lot about resourcefulness in the times of the Polish People's Republic, that is, when I was studying myself and had a good vantage point, because I lived in a student residence, where accommodation was granted to people of modest means. This, however, would interest only few today. Let me just recall that in socialist Poland, university admission was conditional on demonstrating quite considerable knowledge during entrance exams. There were relatively few places in particular majors, much fewer than there were aspirants to become a student. Was that a guarantee that the outstandingly intelligent would be selected? Not necessarily. Social background (working class or peasant) and appeals against negative decisions of the admissions committees were taken into account, though not always with a successful outcome for the candidate. Still, even at that preliminary stage, one had to muster resourcefulness that opened the doors of the university to some and closed them to others. How the former would subsequently fare is a topic for reunions many years later.

I would like to share a little more about student resourcefulness in the so-called free Poland. After all, I was an academic lecturer for five decades and held the positions of vice-director for student affairs, vice-dean and dean of the faculty where several thousand students were educated as part of several different programmes. In the first role, I saw how resourceful they could be when, for example, they found it difficult to pass a course due to absences. They often invoked some illness and were even able produce a doctor's note. Obtaining such a note has never been a problem, not only for the student. However, some managed to get one quite regularly. What did they do during their absences? Extramural students usually had a permanent, paid job. Full-time students, on the other hand, only worked occasionally. At any rate, they showed such resourcefulness that at my former university (AMU) compulsory classes remained only in the senior years of study.

Of course, this did not solve the students' welfare issues. Some of them could be mitigated by scholarships awarded for academic performance and financial benefits if they could prove that the income of their family was too low to contribute anything to their upkeep. As dean, I one dealt with a sociology student who received them on a fairly regular basis, but the direct encounters did not involve her applying for the benefits. Instead, I would meet her when students protested against a solution that they considered inconvenient. It turned out that she was one of the more active participants of the anarchist movement and a resident of the Rozbrat squat, located in one of the abandoned buildings in Poznań. I have no knowledge of her later fates as a student (although I would be surprised if she even completed her undergraduate programme). However, I tend to agree with the singer Maciej Maleńczuk, who said in a TV interview that that mode of 'freeload' living attests to a certain resourcefulness. The student who enrolled year after year for different majors but did not study anywhere, being interested solely in benefits for underprivileged students, was quite resourceful, in a sense. He kept on receiving the benefits until he caused such a fuss at the dean's office that the vice-dean of students took an interest in him and put an end to his resourcefulness. However, it cannot be ruled out that he resurfaced (the 'wobbly doll' way) at another university.

In the so-called free Poland, getting a place in a student hall has never been easy. There places available are relatively few, while students apply numerously to take advantage of the fairly cheap accommodation. The 'miracle formula' of how to repeatedly beat the competition is probably known to the lucky ones themselves and the members of the student committees which, albeit formally supervised by the university authorities and obliged to rely on the income criterion (the lower the family income, the greater the chance of obtaining student housing), have in fact been inclined to adopt criteria that satisfy some and provoke protests from others. Such protests will never lead to a 'miraculous' increase of available accommodation, but they have succeeded in making student housing one of the hottest topics in politics in recent years. The AMU residence in Zwierzyniecka Street in Poznań has received the most publicity. The university authorities tried to 'strike a deal' with the protesters but, besides the fact that the latter did not really want to talk, the problem was that the group included people who had previously studied at Adam Mickiewicz University and others who had never studied there but came from other academic centres to show their dissatisfaction with the material conditions of student life. I did not live in that particular building during my student days; therefore I cannot say much about what student life was like there. However, I have vivid memories of what was my daily abode for several years. Perhaps a similar sentiment was shared by the protesters who already work somewhere or at least should be working. Among other things, I am led to such a conjecture by the example of a student who lived in my hall and, although he studied a little, partying was a priority he enjoyed so much that he continued to do so in other residences a few years after graduating. However, I seriously doubt whether his resourcefulness translates into a role model for the younger generation of students.

Educational resourcefulness

This type of resourcefulness is predicated not only on students' talents, conscientiousness and hard work, but also on their ability to choose the right major, as educational requirements vary from high to lower across the spectrum. Nowadays, admission is no particular challenge; in fact, it is an art not to be accepted at the higher schools which offer a wide range of programmes and where either sensible grade average from secondary school or mere application suffice to enrol. This is also the case in those Western countries where academic studies are paid for by taxpayers. Another favourable circumstance is the opportunity to apply for several different programmes, so that the student who is not accepted at their dream major, may find placement where there are places available. After a while, the student may transfer to a major that is either more appealing or at least easier to study. In effect, one studies to survive until better times and wanders from major to major until the financial resources of the 'itinerant' student have been exhausted. However, certain students have serious difficulties in mastering the material and passing exams already during their first year but still try to meet the educational requirements somehow. They may count on some assistance from the authorities of the faculties which provide remedial classes (is almost a rule in mathematics). Even so, there is little that can be done when serious deficits in terms of secondary school education are compounded by poor intellectual aptitude.

I taught philosophy with numerous, different majors, including the programmes that prospective students flock to every year, such as psychology. The motivations of the candidates vary, but the situation of a graduate in this field is quite alike, that is, the demand for psychologists is not high enough for each to find employment in their profession. However, secondary school graduates should know this before choosing this major, especially since it is a five-year master's programme and cannot be switched to another after obtaining the bachelor's degree. Does it make people who choose this programme less smart than others? I would not say so. Rather, they are people who would like to be specialists in the human soul, but the ideas and notions of what it is may differ. Also, quite many still want to study journalism, in which case most have at least a rough idea of what the job entails. Then again, apart from the specific skillset, it takes plenty of luck in life to land a job as a journalist. As regards law graduates, such luck can be significantly helped by the family and social network of the family members who already practice the profession and hold decision-making positions. In any case, students of the above majors first have to master the content of the curriculum, then face the examiners who are not always lenient towards their weaknesses and finally deal with the supervisors who may but do not have to offer far-reaching help with their theses.

I also gave lectures and conducted exams in philosophy for majors that enjoy less popularity, such as language and literature studies. The students of Romance and Italian philology may have shown considerable linguistic talent but did not have much of a knack for philosophy. A way to tackle the problem had to be found. I suggested that they familiarise themselves with philosophical texts in the languages they studied and, during the exam, I asked them what they had remembered and understood. In my last years at university, I ran a seminar as part of the major called theatre studies. The problem was that the students were not particularly interested in philosophy; in fact, quite a few were mainly interested in what they could find on their smartphones. One hopes those were more serious issues than what gossip websites supply, but that was impossible to verify. Passing the course required a grade entered in the USOS system, but having the students take a serious test to gauge their knowledge could have proved a disaster as well as call the point of including the course in the curriculum into question (meeting the teaching load in philosophy in anything but easy today).

My most extensive experience and insights are associated with teaching students of philosophy. I specialise in modern philosophy, particularly in French and Italian thought. I taught such a course for many years in the second year of philosophy studies, first in the form of compulsory classes and then as a lecture ending with an exam. While I was gaining academic experience, I took those classes so seriously that I expected the students to adopt a fairly serious approach too, which they would demonstrate during the exam. Indeed, some did, so much so that they even went on to become full professors in the humanities, in the discipline of philosophy. However, they were the evident minority. The majority enrolled for philosophy in the belief that it is the study of everything, but rather nothing as specific as, for example, mathematically entangled philosophy of Descartes', or the theologically involved Jansenism of B. Pascal's. Consequently, many of those students struggled terribly during exams. To alleviate their sufferings, I was forced to come up with questions that such a student would be able to answer relatively meaningfully. Obviously, it was not always possible to formulate questions of the kind, and I had no choice but to give a failing grade. I must admit that, over time, I became more and more indulgent towards students' weaknesses, even in those students who believed themselves philosophers but were incapable of mastering academic philosophy. Needless to say, students are not completely defenceless in the fight against lecturers who are too demanding or just inconvenient. One of such 'weapons' is the teacher evaluation survey that the students may complete. In 2024, the dismissal of a philosophy professor who taught in one of the philological programmes at the Adam Mickiewicz University attracted substantial publicity. In their justification, the university authorities invoked the negative ratings in those surveys. This not only prompted protests from the professor in question but also caused some surprise among the academic lecturers who are aware of the motivations which accompany filling such surveys. Some students do wish to express their gratitude for interesting lectures or classes. Others, however, want to vent their anger at having to attend a course like philosophy.

Academic ageing

Old age does not always mean having to look for care and a carer. After all, despite being advanced in years, there are people capable of coping so well as to be the envy of many a younger person. However, much depends on how one has lived and who one was at a younger age. The same goes for academic ageing.

The ageing of institutions

I will start by citing the academy founded by Plato in ancient Athens (in a park dedicated to the hero Akademos), which is where the term 'academy' derives from. In *A History of Ancient Philosophy*, Giovanni Reale claims that the Academy 'was successful very quickly and attracted young men as well as well-known scholars in great numbers'. Also, it soon turned out that the most talented of Plato's students not only did not share their master's teachings but also subscribed to those that meant taking a completely different path in philosophy. Aristotle was one of the most eminent among them, and his authority would be repeatedly invoked in later centuries. Other successors to Platonic philosophy would ensure that their Platonism was not associated with dogmatism but with a scepticism that left no room for dogmatism. However, only a few are willing to concur with the representative of the Third Athenian Academy, Carneades, who asserted that 'all knowledge is impossible, except for the knowledge that all other knowledge is impossible'. On the other hand, many still espouse Plato's understanding of knowledge, while in the book entitled *The Closing of the American Mind*, Allan Bloom even sees a rescue for higher education in the United States – which he believes to be in a state of severe decline (stating in the subtitle that it has 'failed democracy and impoverished the souls of today's students') – in returning to this philosopher. Let us be clear: this would not only mean closing the doors of the academia to women, but also a selection process that would transform the vast majority of academics into either uncritical guardians of philosophers or menial labourers that cannot comprehend philosophers and philosophy.

The Middle Ages saw the emergence of institutions such as church colleges and later universities. Both still exist today. However, it was chiefly the latter that managed to forge values and greatnesses that meant a departure from the ideological supervision of philosophers, theologians and the Churches which supported them. Naturally, this did not happen quickly or so radically that they disappeared from universities without a trace. This becomes quite evident when visiting the oldest of the English higher schools, that is, Cambridge University, founded in 1209. The names of its organisational units still feature such terms as Magdalene College (est. 1428), Jesus College (est. 1496), or Trinity College (est. 1546). However, the adherence to those traditional names is not the only thing that counts, as they do uphold the academic 'spirit' of change that has kept the university at the top of the prestigious Shanghai list of the world's best universities for years. Numerous higher schools in continental Europe also have ecclesiastical lineage, including the Sorbonne which, established in 1253 following the transformation of one of the colleges of the University of Paris, remained a famed academic centre until at least the early twentieth century. Its 1968 'multiplication' into thirteen independent universities in 1968 was due to the fact that its organisational and management structures had aged to such a degree that the school no longer met the modern requirements of its students. Undoubtedly, many of the younger universities would like to age in such a fashion, with people still queuing up to study there.

The ageing of theories

For centuries, scientists have aspired to formulate scientific theories that would stand up to even the most rigorous tests and prove their authors infallible. So far, none of them have succeeded. Even so, we need to keep trying, because these attempts are the driving force behind scientific progress. It is encouraging to note that at least some scientific theories had a relatively long lifespan, such as the heliocentric theory. The idea of the Earth revolving around the Sun was first advanced in the 5th century BC by the Greek philosopher Philolaus of Croton. In the 3rd century BC, it was popularised by Aristarchus of Samos, who 'added' the element of 'central fire' to the theory to account for the Universe. However, it was only the version expounded in Copernicus' *On the Revolutions of the Celestial Spheres* from 1543 that is considered groundbreaking. Has this theory become outdated? In some respects, no, but in others, it has. I do not think any serious scientist today would support the claim that the centre of the universe is 'somewhere near the Sun'. In light of the universe envisioned in Stephen Hawking's *A Brief History of Time*, this notion is downright naive.

The theory of evolution has a long history as well. Its formulation is attributed to Charles Darwin, or at least it is advanced in his 1859 work *On the Origin of Species by Means of Natural Selection*. However, M. White and J. Gribbin state in *Darwin: A Life in Science* that 'Charles Darwin was not the first person to think about evolution' and list such precursors of the theory as Empedocles of Akragas in antiquity (in whose opinion 'plant life arose first after the formation of the Earth, and that animal life "budded off" from the plants'), and Francis Bacon in the modern era ('writing in 1620, more than two hundred years before Darwin set sail on the *Beagle*, and more than three hundred years before the discovery of DNA, Bacon provided as neat a description of the potential of genetic engineering as you could wish to see'). Today, many scientific institutions engage in research in the field of evolutionary biology, and some even invoke Darwin in their very names. However, it would be rather difficult to find an evolutionary biologist there who would subscribe to Darwin's postulation that his theory sufficiently explains the origin and modification of species. Ronald Fisher is one of the scientists who supplement it with Mendelian genetics. Others, such as Richard Dawkins, enhance it with the theory of the 'selfish gene' that replicates and selects individuals in the process of evolution ('all life evolves through the differential survival of replicating individuals'). However one might look at it, the Darwinian theory is one of those that may be scientifically revised and enhanced by theories which simultaneously satisfy the scientific criteria and allow serious polemics with their authors.

Can the same be said of the theories advanced in history as a branch of the humanities? I am not at all certain about that. The generalisations formulated in history do not constitute scientific laws in the strict sense, being historical generalisations that are characterised by limited validity, but that is not the point. More importantly, the generalisations proposed by some historians are questioned by others, who may formulate their own. This stems from a long-standing tradition that dates back to antiquity, which saw historians such as Herodotus of Halicarnassus (whose *Histories* contain generalisations about the Greek, Persian and Egyptian worlds of his time) and Thucydides, author of *History of the Peloponnesian War*. In the Middle Ages, generalisations about the earthly and supernatural realms were presented by Aurelius Augustinus in his *De Civitate Dei*. In the modern times, generalisations about the kings of England and their subjects were put forward by David Hume in the multi-volume *History of England*. Then, the nineteenth century witnessed an 'outpouring' of such works, and at least some competed with each other for the title of the most accurate. The authors attempted to validate them through reference to the same events, but the latter would often be recounted in radically different ways. Today, hardly anyone needs to be persuaded that historical developments are just as relevant in this discipline as the assessments and points of view that historians deemed the most appropriate. As a result, they write their own history. Sometimes it elicits admiration among their readers, and sometimes causes surprise, even outright protests. A number of eloquent examples of such controversial accounts may be found in R. H. Fritze's *Invented Knowledge. False History, Fake Science and Pseudo-Religions*.

The ageing of scholars

Genetics has made such tremendous advances that it is possible to remove the genes which contribute the most to ageing in all living organisms. Unfortunately, the 'immortality gene' has not been discovered yet. Perhaps there are scientists who hope for a breakthrough in this matter. Though immortality remains beyond reach, it is at least feasible to live much longer than the average human life expectancy. After all, there are regions in the world where the number of centenarians far exceeds the statistical average. However, scholars do not happen to live there, as a rule, being only present in such locations study the impact of the natural environment, diet and daily activities on the longevity of the native inhabitants. Most likely, the ancients already realised that a sound diet and physical activity can generally help to prolong life. Nothing is guaranteed, but it may at least be worthwhile to try. In any case, death and taxes are certain and while both can be delayed a little, one should not overdo it. After all, if we manage not to pay all the taxes before we die, our heirs will have to settle the arrears. And if we manage to live to a hundred or even a little more, it may turn out that this old age is unbearable for us and our loved ones alike. I am being somewhat ironic, but only a little, because the issue is so serious that it deserves a few words.

The count of years is not always a reliable indicator of old age. There are people who look and feel much younger than their date of birth would suggest, and others who look and feel much older. Do academics fall into the former category? Sometimes they do, and sometimes they do not. I happen to have met both types on my academic path. If I were to say what has helped them to stay young longer, I would go for prudent approach to scientific activity and the successes thus achieved. Undeniably, it entails high risk of professional failure and so-called burnout, manifesting in an aversion to taking on new tasks, becoming withdrawn and, at best, taking an ironic view of everything and everyone. What A. Einstein used to say towards the end of his life suggests that he suffered from burnout. In the penultimate chapter of his biography, titled *All an Illusion*, R. Highfield and P. Carter quote the words of the scientist, who observed that his contemporaries would consider him an 'old fool', and the physicist Frank Wilczek who, later coming to live in Einstein's Mercer Street house in Princeton, observed that 'all his efforts [in the quest for a satisfactory unified field theory] were fundamentally misconceived. (…) His assistant Bruria Kaufman asked him if everything was comfortable. Einstein replied to her, smiling, "Everything is comfortable. But I am not."' At the time, Einstein was suffering from an aortic aneurysm and could only be spoon-fed ice cubes and mineral water. However, when help of a specialist physician was suggested, he refused and said, 'I want to go when I want'. Obviously, not every scientist can afford to be so self-deprecating. If I mention this example, it is primarily to show that there is no scholar so great as to rise above the inconveniences of old age. Even so, one tries to tackle certain symptoms of old age, such as grumbling about everyone and everything, or expecting loved ones to patiently bear the various mood swings.

I am currently about the same age as Einstein in the situation described above. Do I have a sense of professional burnout? Probably not, or if I do, it is rather a kind of reluctance to keep social contacts with those whom I used to meet quite regularly. Do I feel that the aspirations that motivated my academic activity have been fulfilled? I rather think so. What is more, I am convinced that I have not yet said the last word on the issues I am interested in as a scientist. Naturally, I do not expect any applause from the academic community, whether for my achievements or for this declaration of readiness to continue being academically active.

The recipe for academic success

If I said that I knew a universal recipe for achieving significant academic success, probably few people would believe it, and certainly not those who are well versed in the realities of academic life. However, the point is not so much that I do not know such a recipe (and perhaps no one does), but that there are different paths leading to it, and the one that works in one case does not necessarily work in many others. The point is also that there are different measures of this success.

Difficult paths

In my lectures for doctoral students, speaking about the realities of academic life, I sometimes joke that it would be best to be born a great scientist in this environment. In this way, they would avoid many of the difficulties that still lie ahead. However, this is just a joke, because even those who were born with clear predispositions to conduct scientific research and achieve significant results in it must put in a lot of effort so as not to end up with so-called good promise. Of course, even more must be put in by those who, although they have certain predispositions for this, are neither as great as those of the former, nor so visible that their academic environment decides to grant them a large 'credit' of trust and give them a chance to prove themselves – first in the form of a doctorate they prepare, and later their possible employment at the university. In either case, such candidates for scientists must help themselves and show more than just a desire to extend their academic life through doctoral studies. The relatively low rate of education at this level shows that in many cases there is such a desire, but there is a lack of appropriate work on oneself and one's doctorate.

However, if there are already such desires and such work, then the problem of further barriers to overcome appears. One of the more serious ones is the research problem undertaken. Of course, one should measure intentions by strength. This is easier said than done. Not only because the actual capabilities of such a research novice are often a big mystery, but also the scale of difficulty of the research problem undertaken. This also applies to experienced scientists – just to cite Albert Einstein as an example, who tried for years to solve problems related to gravity, without success. However, there are circumstances that encourage some, while discourage others from undertaking a specific problem. These include, among others, the achievement of successes in it by other, often more experienced scientists. In the case of those fields of science in which team research is the standard, the possibility of making a mistake in choosing a problem is limited by the experience of many scientists involved in solving it (often high-class specialists from various scientific disciplines). However, it does not eliminate it completely. Success achieved by some scientists can be, and often is, a kind of 'driving wheel' for others. It is able to 'speed up' such research to such an extent that it becomes a kind of fashion, and the scientists participating in it try to meet the standards applicable in it.

The emergence of various fashions in science is not always harmful. They can significantly contribute to focusing forces and resources (including financial ones) on solving very serious and important social problems. They become harmful only when they begin to live their own lives or even impose on others a way of thinking about scientific correctness and marginalise those who do not want to or cannot obey them. Such fashions in science – as in other areas of life – come and go. However, before they go, they can not only exploit a research problem long after it has already been solved by serious scientists but even add to it such marginal issues that in the battle for obtaining financial resources for research beat the important ones. Even if such a victory adds some seriousness to them, it is not able to make them very serious.

Such apprentices of scientific research as doctoral students may not even know it. However, their supervisors can tell them about it. The point is, however, that they want to and are able to tell them about it in such a way that they do not get entangled in this game of being a fashionable scientist.

It is probably easier for those who are neither participants in this game, nor do they particularly appreciate those who either 'spin its wheels' or are 'screwed' by it into scientific marginalia. Eventually, a certain sense of reason comes even for those who were a kind of 'showcase' of some fashion in science. However, while for those scientists who already have an established position it may be a reason for jokes, for those who are just aspiring to it may mean the loss of a professional and life opportunity. I will not even try to indicate here a recipe for how to first become fashionable in science and then honourably part with such a label and move on to solving unfashionable but scientifically important problems. There are many ways to achieve both the former and the latter, and the changing realities of academic life will suggest others.

Shortcuts

One such shortcut is following fashion in science. In many cases, it allows for faster and easier finding both the currently discussed research problem and ways of solving it, as well as those who want to participate in this undertaking and contribute something 'from themselves'. However, all this until the point where the fashionable problem and fashionable ways of solving it, or even presenting research results, start to 'eat their own tail' and do so effectively that it eventually becomes a 'stump' whose waving will only impress few, if any. A good example of this is – in my opinion – the current fashion for measuring the value of scientific achievements with the impact factor (IF) determined by the method proposed by Hirsch. There is something astonishing in the fact that what was initially an expression of frustration by this American physicist who felt underestimated by the scientific community and proposed a method of measurement in which his scientific achievements fared well, has become such an international standard which is often approached uncritically – also in those fields and scientific disciplines in which the results are rather difficult to evaluate using such statistics. I am not saying that it says nothing. The point is that it should say more about these results than about manipulating them in such a way that first the list of highly ranked publications would include those in which their publishers have their own commercial interests to take care of, and then they would attract the attention of more or less serious scholars and 'free riders' (because what else can you call those who do not publish in them but support them). Today, this fashion has admittedly 'eaten a bit of its own tail', but for now it cannot be said that only a 'stump' remains of it. However, I hope that the currently indicated imperfections of the impact factor will eventually lead to this. In any case, this discussion shows, convincingly enough, that those who want to count in science, even if they take such a shortcut, should know at what point to leave it and enter one that may be out of fashion, but may still give a greater chance of achieving more reliable indicators in science.

Much depends on what is considered important in academic life. It would be rather difficult to defend the claim that the most important thing for the vast majority of the academic community is conducting scientific research and achieving significant results in it. This is contradicted not only by various statistical indicators for these results, but also by the so-called academic reality visible to the naked eye. Of course, it looks different not only in different countries, but also in the same country, but at different universities, and even at the same university, but in different fields and disciplines. Apart from anything else, it is a confirmation that the Pareto principle, that is, 20% to 80%, is still valid in the academic environment. However, these 20% of people with above-average qualifications and above-average commitment to research work differ significantly at the world's leading universities from the 20% at second- or third-rate universities. The same is true for this 80%. A large part of it consists of people whose role comes down to – in the better version – cheering on the scientists who stand out with their qualifications and the results obtained in their research work, and in the worse version, to letting them know that they are not as good professionally as they think, or at least that they are still far from scientific perfection.

The problem is not that these 'fans' are completely wrong (after all, perfection takes years to achieve), and not even that they only do destructive 'work' (often such a pursuit of perfection must be accompanied by suffering), but that they are able to create such barriers that it is very difficult for many above-average scholars to cross, and sometimes they are forced to look for a place for themselves where these average people do not have so much to say. It is not possible to briefly answer the question: how do these average people gain such a significant position at the university that their voice translates into these difficulties? There are many ways to do this. Only one of them is to obtain the position of university decision-maker, such as the position of rector, dean or director of the institute. According to the standards and legal regulations in force in the academic environment, these are obtained in democratic elections. Already in the nineteenth century, John Stuart Mill, in his treatise *Liberalism*, pointed out the existence of a 'mechanism' in democracy that makes mediocrity vote for mediocrity, which in some cases leads to the former entrusting their fate to those he calls 'vulture kings'. He added, however, that 'without such a vulture king, the common vultures would peck each other' Perhaps in academic life it is more difficult for such 'vultures' to get a say, or at least they do not have such a wide field to show off their 'beak'. However, if they do get a chance, they can give many a serious scholar a 'cheer'. What I mean by this is that democracy does not always work in academic life. It is important not only to approach democracy critically, but also not to come 'on your knees' to those who can help us in something, or to those who can harm us in something.

Personal experiences

Today, the fashion for presenting a group of scholars gathered around a master or a scientific school has lost some of its popularity. In the past century, however, it enjoyed considerable popularity and even caused such groups to go down in the history of science. In Poland during the interwar period, one of them was a group of philosophers called the Lvov-Warsaw school. It brought together various people, including those who later successfully continued their academic careers in Western countries. Some of them remained in Poland and after 1945, they clashed with representatives of the new 'school' that Marxism wanted to be recognised as. This confrontation turned out to be quite painful for many of them (to mention only Kazimierz Ajdukiewicz and Władysław Tatarkiewicz as examples). The point is not that they did not have their own arguments, but that their opponents used in this confrontation the criticism that Tadeusz Kotarbiński called 'police-like'; it comes down to 'just looking for some loophole to ruin someone'. Leszek Kołakowski (in his youth a militant supporter of Marxism) recalled it in his lecture delivered in 1992 on the occasion of his alma mater (University of Łódź) awarding him an honorary doctorate. He admitted that in those years it seemed to him – like to many other Marxists – that he was 'all-knowing'; and it is rather impossible to seriously argue with someone like that in science.

I will say immodestly that during my academic youth, this 'school', fashionable in Poland at the time, did not make such a great impression on me to want to follow the teachings of its masters and teachers or even to take a serious interest in their 'omniscience'. At that time, the seventeenth century French philosophy, quite distant from Marxism, seemed much more interesting and fascinating to me, especially its representatives such as Blaise Pascal and Descartes (I have published more than one monograph on their views). I was also very lucky in life and at work, because my immediate superior at that time was indeed a declared Marxist, but with disarming honesty admitted that he knew nothing about what I was doing, and not only did he not hinder me in continuing my research, but he was also deeply convinced that I would manage on my own. Of course, it is not up to me to judge how I managed and am managing in it. I am aware, however, that the long and problematically diverse list of my publications may be irritating to some of those who judge my achievements. However, I cannot promise them that I will not add more items to it.

Academic bureaucracy

Few people would associate bureaucracy with something positive, even with the ennobling attribute 'academic' attached to it. More often than not, it brings to mind officials who treat the customers and applicants in a manner which shows them who is in charge. While the first component of that term denotes an office (or a desk), the second one (Gr. *kratos*) already means power; and what kind of power would it be if it did not harbour a sense of its importance and superiority over ordinary citizens? This is often the case in the academia.

Bureaucratic typology

Such a classification was advanced as early as the eighteenth century, that is, at a time when the concept was introduced into public circulation (by Vincent de Gournay). In the following century, it played a significant role in Alexis de Tocqueville's *Democracy in America*, as the author discussed social behaviours thanks to which the eponymous democracy proves superior to various types of despotisms and despots (not only of the clerical kind). However, it was not until the early twentieth century that it was thoroughly analysed, for instance by Max Weber, who described the diverse manifestations and types of bureaucracy. In his seminal *Economy and Society*, Weber discussed its Chinese, Egyptian and European varieties, at different stages of economic and political development. Naturally, no bureaucracy could do without bureaucrats, who feature frequently in Weber's work, not only in their official capacity (although the latter is particularly emphasised). It follows that such a bureaucrat-official is subject exclusively to objective official duties, and of course to those who establish them, control their performance and, in case of any misconduct, can deprive the official of their place at their desk with one signature. Hence, the official hangs on tightly to their desk and will be profoundly interested in making both their duties and their guardians 'immortal' (as Weber puts it). Robert Merton's later analyses of bureaucrat behaviour revealed such social pathologies as 'learned ineptitude', 'occupational psychosis', ritualism and conformism. They may also be encountered in the operation of academic bureaucracy and the academic bureaucrat. The fact was noted by M. Weber in his 1917 lecture *Science as a Vocation* where, among other things, he criticised the bureaucratic model of the American university, in which the head of an institute resembles the directors of 'all capitalist and at the same time bureaucratised enterprises', believing that 'this institute is "his", and he manages its affairs', and if any of the subordinates does not like the arrangement, they may start looking for another job.

Central bureaucracy

Although a whole century has passed since M. Weber delivered the aforementioned lecture, any significant change in academic bureaucracy has been for the worse rather than for the better, at American universities and elsewhere. I have heard that in many higher schools, power does not lie in the hands of the vice-chancellors, presidents or deans, but is held by the officials, without whose benevolence one can live, but what kind of life is that? European universities, of course, have their own clerical traditions, but a substantial number yield to the behest of EU or national politicians and officials (and often both) to implement the inventions of the Brussels bureaucrats whose academic experience is frequently confined to their studies (nonetheless, they believe they know best what is good for universities). What I mean to say is that today, central bureaucracy extends beyond the ministerial tier to encompass European Union offices that set the standards of academic correctness. Of course, attempts may be made to play it all down, but then one must expect to wake up without the means to conduct world-class research and without the prestige of participating in international academic life and, consequently, involvement in research projects whose cost estimates can make many a national planner dizzy.

In the countries of the European Union, local ministerial bureaucracy also has a say, even at its lower tiers. I had the opportunity to experience this first-hand when working on a research project funded by the Committee for Scientific Research – a central government agency – and had to deal with bureaucrats (in the rank of senior specialist) who had seen multiple political parties and ministers come and go. Naturally, the roles are divided in every bureaucracy – including the ministry. The role of the minister can be devolved to the deputies or even department directors. After all, the minister cannot handle everything and sometimes even say what they really think (owing the position to politics and politicians). This is not just about delegating one of the officials to read the minister's congratulation letter at a university celebration, but also about using the opportunity to say what might be awkward coming from the minister themselves. The participants of the formal sitting of the academic senates of Poznań to celebrate their centennial may guess which address that was. For those who did not attend, I will only say that although universities face rather trying times, they are not so difficult that the rector of a major university should not have the courage to say what the parliamentary opposition says and what a large proportion of the public is convinced of. I am not going to quote the former rector of my university here, as I could be accused of trying to ingratiate myself with him. Instead, I will say something that is common knowledge, but which the ministry officials sometimes seem to forget. They are appointed to their offices only to leave, sooner or later. However, the consequences of their not entirely thought-out actions often persist for so long that hardly anyone will remember who was responsible.

A once popular saying claimed that 'one who has not served at sea knows nothing of life'. Adapting it in line with the eponymous issue, we could say that 'one who has not dealt with university bureaucracy knows nothing of academic life'; the longer the exposure, the more one can see that such bureaucracy has its 'philosophy' of operating and surviving behind the desk, so as to make it through the biggest university revolutions. This applies less to the university officials who – just as like rectors, deans or institute directors – were appointed to their positions (at least until the introduction of Act 2.0 in 2018) by the vote of the university community, but it is much more true for the individuals hired at the request of heads of organisational units at the university. Still, I could share much about that first group of university officials, too, having made numerous observations over the course of several decades of academic life. Some of those insights tally with the fairly common belief that any power corrupts, while great power (including university authority) corrupts even more profoundly (against which professorial titles offer little protection). Well, corrupt it may, but it does not have to. Having worked many years at a university and 'coexisted' with various rectors, deans and institute directors, I met a few who let power go so much to their heads that in many respects they seemed an embodiment of Weber's 'director-dictator'. Some, on the other hand, may not have been able to strew the path with flowers for everyone, but at least sought to live in harmony with all. Unfortunately, performing responsible university roles in this manner is impossible, though any such authority may be expected not to elevate itself too much above other members of the academic community, or at least not to surround itself with a 'court' of sycophants. This, however, varies as well, and I do not think I am alone in this belief. In my opinion, many universities have their share of officials who behaved or behave as if the university, faculty or institute belonged to them. Simultaneously, I am convinced that this does not particularly benefit the institutions they work for. This observation is relevant insofar as the new laws applicable to universities in Poland have granted considerable powers to the rectors, while the Minister of Education and Science has publicly deplored that they often voluntarily relinquish some of them.

Rectors, deans and heads of organisational units are just one facet of the university bureaucracy. In their day-to-day functioning, the university community is more affected by interaction with the administrative staff whose authority is exercised from the level of their official desk. I certainly do not wish to underestimate their role in academic life, even if it is limited to examining a document and applying (or not) their official stamp to it. After all, the rank-and-file officials know, or at least should know, how such a document should be drawn up and when it should be submitted. Now, they only become a real bureaucrat at the point when they consider this knowledge to be a sufficient grounds for treating petitioners (never mind whether or not they hold professorial titles) as if they were not smart enough to keep up with various regulations. The approach to the applicants in important university positions may be the exception (but does not have to be). After all, a bureaucrat is possessed of a self-preservation instinct and has a rough idea of who can be looked down upon and who should be reckoned with; if this instinct fails as them, they may have to look for another desk. As a former dean, there is much I could say on that subject. However, it would not be 'in keeping with the times' since the aforementioned regulations have deprived deans of a number of important powers while empowering rectors so much that one is 'afraid to be scared'.

A few suggestions

Attempts to show how to deal with the nuisances of bureaucracy have already been made, but I do not think they are universal enough to fit every situation in which a bureaucrat treats their clients as necessary evil. A. Tocqueville's aforementioned vision of American democracy offers one such example. I am inclined to argue that the alternative of 'either democracy or bureaucracy' formulated by that author has a rather limited validity. Without much difficulty, one can find instances in which democracy strengthens bureaucracy and bureaucracy reinforces democracy (today's functioning of the organisational structures of the European Union is just one of them). At universities, this alliance of democracy and bureaucracy has its own peculiar traits, not only because they are essentially hierarchical, but also due to specialisation which prevents scholars from competently performing the professional tasks of the university administration (which, of course, makes the former dependent on the latter). Naturally, academics can readily learn how to carry out administrative duties, but that would come (and does come) at the expense of scientific research.

Even so, certain general suggestions may be advanced (although there is no guarantee that they will be effective). The first is that if we cannot do without bureaucracy, let us at least try to maintain not so much the so-called peace of mind (which may sometimes be very difficult), but exercise understanding for the learned and natural inadequacies of university officials, perhaps even the ineptitude of those who should have seen to our affair but failed to, and there is little that can be done about it (just as with the lost coat in the film by Stanisław Bareja). Secondly, if we want something done quickly and well, we should do it ourselves; and if we do not have the time or inclination to do it, we should blame ourselves and not be surprised that the bureaucrat will treat us as a 'special needs' client (if they actually will, because things may be much worse). Finally, one could perhaps try and transform the learned ineptitude of the bureaucrat into learned professional resourcefulness. This may seem like a utopian idea, but there are countries in Europe where some success in this field has been achieved (I had the opportunity to see this for myself during my travels). Unfortunately, Poland is not one of them yet.

The power of autobiography and biography

Of course, one can be remembered in different ways by one's immediate and distant surroundings. The problem is that we would like to be remembered in the best possible light and for as long as possible. Many people have such expectations, including scholars who have had significant achievements in science. This record can (but does not have to) be served by various autobiographies and biographies. In this part of my considerations, I will mention only a few of those that interested me and prompted deeper reflections; there were more.

The power of autobiography

Writing autobiographies has such a long tradition that today we can say with great conviction that this method of recording oneself in the memory of posterity has been relatively well tested. Few people today would remember that Julius Caesar waged a 7-year war with the Gallic (Celtic) tribes if he had not written his famous memoirs On *The Gallic War*. The fact that he gave them the form of a simple, 'soldierly' account not only of military struggles, but also of the courage and customs of these peoples meant that they found recognition not only among his supporters, but also his fierce opponents (such as Cicero). Their popularity may also have been influenced by the fact that he spoke in the third person (despite having an ego as large as his great empire). There was no shortage of such talented autobiographers in science either. They did not always take the form of memoirs. In the times when the epistolary art reached its peak, they often appeared as letters to friends as well as to people who were simply curious about how such a scholar was doing in science and everyday life, and what advice he could possibly give them. This type of autobiography enjoyed considerable popularity in the seventeenth and eighteenth centuries, and from the letters of philosophers and scholars such as Descartes (he wrote several hundred of them) one can learn a lot not only about what he thought about, among other things, the Copernican theory of the heavens, but also about those who criticised it and persecuted its supporters.

In the nineteenth century, Charles Darwin's theory of the evolution of species was a subject of considerable controversy – he presented it in a book published in 1859 entitled *On the Origin of Species by Means of Natural Selection*. On the other hand, he presented his intellectual path in *Recollections of the Development of My Mind and Character*, written in 1876 for his family. However, he wrote it not only with his family in mind, but also for many who would like to know what contributed to his scientific success and what his views were on many life issues. The last chapter of these memoirs was written by his son Francis Darwin, who was also a valued naturalist (he conducted experimental research on phototropism), and after his father's death prepared his autobiography and correspondence for publication (they were published under the titles *The Life and Letters of Charles Darwin* (1887) and *More Letters of Charles Darwin* (1905). Thanks to these publications, this scientist lost nothing of his scientific greatness and gained a lot as a person who struggled with the same problems that ordinary people struggle with.

Today, there are many more opportunities to present oneself in the most favourable light possible than in the past. Public and private media, including television, have entered the game of gaining the interest and recognition of as many people as possible, without which it would be difficult for those curious about the world to function. The problem is that it is relatively easy to appear on the television screen and to disappear from it. Sometimes it is enough to formulate a life question in front of the camera, and later it will make at least a national career. The problem is that such questions are often remembered longer than those who asked them. Those who try to write themselves into it with long interviews have a longer life in the memory of different people. However, this form of autobiography requires such mastery of the art of telling about oneself that it does not come out that in this miserable world there was and is no one more important than us and possibly those who have contributed to us in some way, because such interviews will probably interest few people. This requires not only a great deal of distance from oneself, but also an interlocutor who will not impose his opinion or at least will not remind us of what we are reluctant to admit publicly. However, we must reckon with the fact that there are still such witnesses to our lives who perceive and evaluate them differently. Despite these and other dangers, such autobiography enjoys considerable popularity today, and long interviews have proliferated like mushrooms after rain. This applies especially to those politicians who have already had their five minutes in politics and have many years of explaining the mistakes they have made or are being attributed in the life ahead of them. Of course, not all of them have achievements on the scale of Caesar or Churchill, or even their talent for telling stories about themselves and others in such a way that their autobiographies will interest many people. How do great scientists find their place in it? It cannot be said that each of them is as good at it as in scientific research. Some of them, however, succeeded so well that they were remembered as people struggling not so much with scientific problems as with their illness. An example of this is the British physicist Stephen Hawking.

The power of biographies

Writing biographies of various people also has a long tradition. In many cases, such people wanted to come out much better in them than their biographers presented. However, there was little they could do at the time, when their images were drawn many years after their death by those who neither knew them personally nor had such accounts that would make the image they drew credible. This is the case, for example, with the image of Pythagoras, who lived at the turn of the 6th and 5th centuries BC, by Porphyry, who lived in the 3rd century AD. Students in schools learn that the former was a great mathematician. On the other hand, from Porphyry's *The Life of Pythagoras* they could learn (if they reached for this biography) that he was also a 'magician' who was able to reverse an epidemic and restrain winds and hail, calm river and sea waves. *Lives of Eminent Philosophers*, drawn 'in bulk' by Diogenes Laertius, may also arouse mixed feelings. Although the image of Plato is still somewhat defensible (despite the fact that this famous philosopher 'fell in love with a certain young man named Aster' and wrote him love epigrams), it would be more difficult to defend the image of his teacher Socrates (because he not only dressed sloppily, but was also accused of 'impiety and corrupting the youth'). For the sake of clarity, I will add that these philosophers lived at the turn of the 5th and 4th centuries BC), and the author of these biographies at the turn of the 2nd and 3rd centuries AD. I am not citing here any of the images that were drawn at that time for politicians of the time, nor those that were drawn for martyrs for the faith. There were so many of them that it would be difficult to find a convincing criterion for their selection that would not offend someone's beliefs and feelings. I will add, however, that the authors of the Gospels can also be considered such biographers. However, this opens up a wide field for discussion as to which of these accounts is closest to the truth, because they diverge in many respects. However, it is beyond discussion that their power of influence on human beliefs and ideas about God and the world was enormous, because without them Christianity would not have become a world religion.

After the era of such great philosophers that their views are still recalled today, and the era of such great theologians that more than one of them was raised to church altars, came the era of such biographers who wrote biographies on political commission. One of the masters in this field was the Florentine writer and philosopher Niccolò Machiavelli. He gained wide publicity with his work *The Prince*. The prototype of the titular prince is the son of Pope Alexander VI, Cesare Borgia. The fact that this work was placed on the church's index of forbidden books in 1559 was not so much because its author 'washed' the dirty papal linen in public, but because it glorified such virtues contrary to the teachings of the Church as the ability to seize power by deceit and to exercise it by means of lies and violence. Machiavelli did not do the prince any favours with it (he ended his adventurous life in prison), but it served as an inspiring reading for those rulers who acted in a similar way to him – such as the Prussian king Frederick II the Great. This ruler was also able to take care of his own image. He invited to his court such writers who were willing and able to express their admiration for him, not only at the royal table, but also in letters to him. One of them was Voltaire (those interested should see the published collection of letters by this philosopher). One could of course ask: how is he not ashamed to speak so well of this ruler, who dealt with his opponents, including Poles, quite unceremoniously? The problem is that this biographer was ashamed of little, and yet he had many such apologetic achievements to his credit, some of which have even entered the history of literature.

Can biographies of scientists written by those who knew them personally count on such a career? So far, none of them have been so successful. However, I know of at least a few that, in my opinion, deserve wider interest. I would include the biography written by Jane Hawking (Stephen Hawking's first wife) entitled: *Travelling to Infinity: My Life with Stephen*. You can learn a lot from it about this outstanding physicist not only from the period of his intellectual maturity, but also from the period in which he was just reaching it. In both periods, he had a high self-esteem for his qualifications, but in the earlier period, it required a lot of understanding from his closest circle. The author of this biography recalled in it that he had convinced her that only fools studied medieval Spanish poetry (she studied it at the University of London and later obtained a doctorate in this field). Another such biography is *Niels Bohr's Times*, written by his direct student and collaborator Abraham Pais. Its author has outlined in an interesting way not only the scientific, but also the personality profile of this outstanding scientist (a Nobel Prize winner in physics). He based this on the observations he had gathered first as his student and later as his long-term collaborator. There are fragments in it that may cause amusement in some readers, but deeper reflection in others. An example of this is those in which Pais recalls a lecture of his during which he suddenly stopped drawing a graph on the blackboard and spent a long time silently wondering what should be included in the next part of it. On the other hand, a peculiar curiosity may be that after intellectually exhausting scientific discussions, he found respite in enthusiastically cultivating a garden.

A lot of interesting information about outstanding scientists can also be found in some biographies, written not on the basis of direct contacts with them, but on collected documents. One of the more successful ones, in my opinion, is the biography entitled *The Private Life of Albert Einstein*. Its co-authors – Roger Highfield and Paul Carter – state in the introduction that, 'caw have been hundreds of books that popularise the theory of relativity and many biographies that have dealt with the life of Albert Einstein. With only one or two exceptions, all portray him as he would have wanted – as an individual who turned his back on personal matters to seek scientific enlightenment'. I cannot answer the question whether this was actually the state of Einsteinian biography before this book was written. However, I can say with great conviction that it shows this scientist not only in his emotional ecstasies and disappointments, but also in such media entanglements that made him a sage for the mass media, whose opinion the whole world sought. For the world of science, this media commotion around him was such a burden that no scientist could bear – because how could they bear the expectation of the so-called general public that some theory could be the 'key to all the secrets of the Universe'. According to *The New York Times*, however, it was supposed to be 'Einstein's new theory of relativity'. Although in a letter to his son Hans Albert, this scientist called it complete idiocy, 'the milk has already been spilled' – if that is how one can say about his finding himself under pressure from the media, which sometimes, even in good faith (but without the proper knowledge), attributed to him such achievements that were beyond his reach.

There is probably no single convincing answer to the question of what motivates the authors of various biographies to create images of great scientists. However, it can be said that if they are already visible in this 'sky' where the real stars of science shine, then they are something like such planets orbiting around them, which 'shine' with reflected light. They may indeed 'warm up' a bit by them, and sometimes even flash something, but they are no longer the 'light rays' that these stars of science emit. However, they can also 'burn' themselves – especially when they want to be considered experts who know better than the scientist presented in the biography what was most important in his life.

Academic publicism

Although publicism is also practiced by numerous academics, it is mainly appreciated by those who no longer have to seek academic promotions, since the activity is not, or at least should not be, taken into account when assessing one's scholarly output. It is a shame, in a way, yet I do not wish to 'plead' for those affected. Instead, I would like to talk about two forms of publicism, namely the engaged and the documentary modality.

Engaged publicism

In English and French, terms such as publicist, *publiciste* are used interchangeably with journalist or *journaliste*. This is due to the long-standing and close links stemming from such a manner of practicing publicism which makes it difficult to distinguish from journalism. Most likely, the lecturers in journalism majors discuss a range of its types with students. However, even ordinary 'consumers' of journalistic merchandise will recognise that business journalism differs from its political or investigative variety. The more inquisitive can also distinguish between journalism that is committed to – or engaged in – science and academic teaching and mere documenting the events and developments in that domain. Still, the boundaries between them have invariably been fluid, and whether or not the person practicing it has an academic degree or title can be confusing, especially today, when so many journalists try to 'step into the shoes' of scholars, and so many scholars try to 'act the part' of journalists. This confusion of roles is not infrequently harmful to science. Whether it is also damaging to journalism is difficult to answer conclusively. In this respect, one could of course draw on tradition, such as the *Journal des sçavans*, founded in 1665, later renamed to *Journal des savans*, and now published as *Journal des savants*. The periodical has featured texts that are still recognised today (such as Ole Rømer's 1676 paper on the speed of light), as well as texts that attest to pseudoscience being confounded with science. An example of the latter is the 1684 account of the French physician and traveller François Bernier, entitled *A New Division of the Earth, according to the Different Species or Races of Men who Inhabit It* (in which one can find a foretaste of the racism that took shape in later centuries). Many more examples of this kind could readily be cited. It is not that publicism should not be committed to a cause, but that the imagination of the publicists should stretch as far as to foresee the disastrous consequences of siding with such causes that may sometimes seem quite innocent at first but reveal their worst facets later.

Today, this is easier in some respects and, simultaneously, much more difficult in others. It is easier because we live in the internet age, where the so-called social media enjoy great popularity. The difficulty, on the other hand, is that the so-called regular citizen must often rely on their own competence and preference when choosing the media to use. The latter, vying to attract the broadest audience possible, use various means in this struggle, including half-truths and outright lies. Thus, the new category of 'fake news' has been coined to describe false information which is disseminated deliberately in social media to win over as many people as possible. Research is being conducted to measure public trust in various types of information outlets. According to a 2021 study by the Pew Research Centre, as many as 84% of Americans use such media, and more than 20% declared considerable confidence in those platforms. Furthermore, numerous analyses have also been concerned with the communicated content. It turns out that social media serve to spread various conspiracy theories and false information to 'whitewash' some people and smear others. One such notorious case was a fabricated email from Hillary Clinton, released by a non-existent newspaper, *The Denver Guardian*, with the aim of damaging the political reputation of the US presidential candidate. Poland, of course, has its own experts in defaming some and whitewashing others. However, naming anyone specific will immediately cause their defenders to step forward.

Even so, I will cite at least one example of backbiting that involves the academic community. In July 2024, *Tygodnik Powszechny* featured an article by

Anna Golus entitled 'The Dean Can do Anything'. Online, it may be found under a more sensational title, that is, 'Nepotism at the Naval Academy in Gdynia: it should serve defence instead of protecting the dean's relatives from unemployment'. The text alleged that 'the Ministry of National Defence finances educational studies and religious research at the Naval Academy. It also pays for the positions of the dean's relatives employed there. And the dean collects points for publications in scientific journals in which he is the editor'. The individual thus described is Prof Jerzy Kojkoł, dean of the Faculty of Humanities and Social Sciences at the Academy. I know him personally and have repeatedly accepted his invitations to participate in scientific congresses and conferences held at that university. I cannot confirm that he 'can do anything', but I can list facts which demonstrate that he has done a lot of good for his faculty; for instance, he has succeeded in having Education Studies there recognised as category A programme in parameterisation. The author of the article also questioned Kojkoł's academic qualifications, but following a procedure carried out in 2024, the Commission for Scientific Excellence found that he met the requirements for professorship and motioned the President to award the title. However, the most astonishing allegations are that the Academy also offers studies in education and that the dean engages with religious studies, among other things. It would appear that the author of the article entertains thoroughly wrong notions about the range of programmes available at Polish higher schools and the scope of scientific interests of the scholars who have the status of independent researchers. This is even more surprising given that the author is not only a university graduate but also obtained a doctorate. Admittedly, neither did she study journalism nor receive the degree in this discipline, but this is no excuse. Even such a casual 'investigative journalist' should know that there are codes of professional ethics for journalists, who should adhere to guidelines such as 'accuracy, objectivity, impartiality, honesty and responsibility for one's words', not to mention the 'trifle' of not publicising the names of persons who have not been duly convicted.

Documentary publicism

This genre can be both beneficial and detrimental to science. However, research reports or overviews of findings seem to enjoy the greatest popularity in the academia. Although the latter would even aspire to pass for a scientific publication, they will not qualify as long as they fail to contribute anything new to science. At least, such was the viewpoint of those who drafted the statutory requirements for candidates for the postdoctoral degree and professorship. These provisions should, ideally, be enforced by those who assess the achievements of applicants in promotion procedures, but their actual application is another matter entirely. Still, I would like to say a few words about the documentary publicism that is practiced by non-scholars who often appear in television paradocumentaries as pundits who comment on what is being shown on the screen. Their names are often accompanied by information (especially in English-speaking channels) that they are writers and journalists, while what they say is supposed to prove that they are well versed in the matter. However, what they say is just as important as how they say it, since they often speak as if they knew more about what is presented on the screen than many a scholar. Nonetheless, besides having no academic status, they often address issues which are of little concern for present-day science, because they are considered either pseudoscientific or impossible to ascertain given the current state of knowledge. Examples include life on other planets or the presence of beings from other planets on Earth. The popularity of such shows is one thing, but one cannot ignore the fact that one of such 'documentarians', writer and publicist Erich A. P. von Däniken, drew considerable interest of the audience with his theory of alien visits to Earth. In *Chariots of the Gods?*, he claims that the geometric lines in the Nazca desert in Peru are the work of beings who once came to Earth. Obviously, the theory has been disputed by academic scholars (Samuel Rosenberg called it a 'gigantic hoax'), but it sold exceedingly well (with over 63 million copies purchased). Still, the journalistic skill alone will not suffice to achieve such a success – it cannot be done without the sensationalist media to back one up. Although the skillset is often lacking, the media are numerous enough – otherwise such sensations would fade faster than they appear.

Less talented documentarians, however, live a much more modest life. Sometimes they have to content themselves with the interest of onlookers who are willing to come to their historical re-enactments, and sometimes they have to settle for their own company. Obviously, this does not mean that these historical reconstructions are worthless. For my part, I consider them to be harmless, and they do give us an idea of how our ancestors lived. Still, it is important that such re-enactors do not consider themselves more knowledgeable than professional historians about the life of centuries ago, while those scholars should not confuse the role of historians with the role of assistants to politicians who know everything best. Apparently, this has been a problem, at least for some of them. In *Invented Knowledge*, Ronald H. Fritze cites the examples of historians who put forward theories claiming that the original inhabitants of America were not 'red-skinned' but white. They were supposed to have settled in North America in ancient times and built a 'glorious civilisation whose sole remains were the many mounds scattered across the eastern United States. Tragically the savage ancestors of the Red Indians (Native Americans) invaded the land of the white men and destroyed the mound-builders'. In Polish historical realities, one of the events whose accounts differ radically is the Katyń massacre of over 21,000 Polish officers and other 'enemies of the people'. When I was a student, I would hear that it was perpetrated by the Germans on Hitler's orders. However, even back then, the more inquisitive historians, politicians and journalists already knew that the Russians had done it on Stalin's orders.

Documentary publicism is also practiced in many milieu periodicals, though its quality varies across the titles. Those which have gained nationwide reputation owe it to the editors and authors who have the courage to address even the most controversial issues and discuss them while taking little heed of the opinion of the individuals they portray in a much less favourable light than the latter would like. However, there are relatively few such magazines in Poland, including *Forum Akademickie*, published in Lublin by a relatively independent publishing house. Even that magazine still has to reckon with the fact that overly harsh or one-sided criticism of the political authorities may deprive the magazine of a ministerial subsidy. If so, what are the editors of the numerous university periodicals supposed to say, given that they are employed by the university? Although they do not necessarily live in constant fear of the wrath of the rectorate, there is something to it. Otherwise, there would be fewer texts in the manner of reports and more critical articles concerning the university administration. In any case, I seriously doubt whether the people whose texts are featured there practice publicism as opposed to 'informationism', merely reporting on the goings-on at the university.

I have only sporadically expressed any views in *Życie Uniwersyteckie*, the magazine of my former university. If anything I stated was published there, it was invariably associated with my role as dean. On the other hand, I have long been active in the *Forum Akademickie* monthly, contributing regularly to each issue since 2018. I did not really volunteer for this, as it was the editor-in-chief Piotr Kieraciński who suggested I do it. Do I find it tiresome? So far, not really. I also derive some satisfaction from the fact that I am appreciated by the editors of that periodical and the people who inform me that they read my column with interest.

Bibliography

Abelard P., (1994), *Logica Ingredientibus, Commentary of Porphyry's Isagoge. Five Texts on the Medieval Problem of Universals: Porphyry, Boethius, Abelard, Duns Scotus, Ockham*. Indianapolis: Hackett.

Abelard, P. (1995), *Peter Abelard: Ethical Writings.*, Indianapolis: Hackett.

Augustine of Hippo (1998), *The City of God against the Pagans*. New York: Cambridge University Press.

Abelard & Héloïse (2007), *The Letters and other Writings*. Indianapolis: Hackett.

Bell B. I., (1929), *Beyond Agnosticism*, New York and London: Harper & Brothers.

Berger P, Th. Luckmann, (1966), *The Social Construction of Reality: A Treatise in the Sociology of Knowledge*, New York: Anchor Books.

Bernier F. (1684), *A New Division of the Earth* (from Journal des Scavans, April 24, 1684), Translated by T. Bendyshe in Memoirs Read Before the Anthropological Society of London, vol. 1, 1863–64, pp. 360–64.

Białas A. *Krzyk rozpaczy* (*A Cry of Despair*). no. 715/2025 PAUza

Bloom A. (1987), *The Closing of the American Mind*. New York: Simon & Schuster.

Bologna declaration, Archived 31 March 2022 at the Wayback Machine magna-charta.org

Carnap R. (1967), *The Logical Structure of the World. Pseudoproblems in Philosophy*, California: University of California Press.

Darwin Ch. (2008), *On the Origin of Species by Means of Natural Selection, or the Preservation of Favoured Races in the Struggle for Life*, London: John Murray.

Darwin Ch. (1958), *The Autobiography of Charles Darwin 1809–1882*. London: Collins

Darwin Ch. (1985), *The Correspondence of Charles Darwin*, Cambridge: Cambridge University Press.

Dawkins R. (2006), *The God Delusion. Boston: Houghton Mifflin.*

Déclaration des droits de l'homme et du citoyen [archive], sur Musée Carnavalet – Histoire de la ville de Paris, 17 mai 2011 (consulté le 24 août 2020).

Descartes R. (2006), *A Discourse on the Method of Correctly Conducting One's Reason and Seeking Truth in the Sciences*, Oxford: Oxford University Press.

Descartes R. (2008), *Meditations on First Philosophy: With Selections from the Objections and Replies*, Oxford: Oxford University Press.

Descartes R. (1983), *Principles of Philosophy*, Dordrecht: Reidel.

Diogenes Laertius (2020), *Lives of Eminent Philosophers., Cambridge: Cambridge University Press.*

Ecklund E. H. (2010), *Science vs. Religion. What Scientists Really Think*, Oxford: University Press.

Einstein A. *Ideas and Opinions*, New York: Crown, 1982 [1954]); originally appeared in the New York Times Magazine, November 9, 1930, 1–4.

Einstein A. (1930), *What I Believe*, Forum and Century (1930–194). New York: Macauley.

Einstein A., Infeld L. (1938), *The Evolution of Physics: The Growth of Ideas from Early Concepts to Relativity and Quanta*, Cambridge: Cambridge University Press.

Einstein S. N. (1992), *Jewish Civilisation: The Jewish Experience in Comparative Perspective*, Albany: Suny Press.

Erasmus Desiderius (2015), *The Praise of Folly*, Princeton: Princeton University Press.

Frankenberry N. K., (2008), *The Faith of Scientists in their own Words*, Princeton and Oxford: Princeton University Press.

Freud Z. (2021), *The Psychopathology of Everyday Life*, London: Penguin Books.

Galileo Galilei (1967), *The Dialogue Concerning the Two Chief World Systems*, Berkeley and Los Angeles: University of California Press.

Gibbon E. (2026), *The autobiography and correspondence of Edward Gibbon, the historian*, Kiel: Hansebooks.

Gobineau A. (1933), *Essai sur l'inégalité des Races humaines*, (1854), Éd.

Gould S. J., (1981), The mismeasure of man, New York: W. W. Norton & Company.

Grant M., (1916), *The Passing of the Great Race, or the Racial Basis of European History*, New York.

Gross N., Simmons S., *The religiosity of American college and University professors*, 'Sociology and Religion' no. 2/70.

Grünbaum A. (1985), *The Foundations of Psychoanalysis: A Philosophical Critique*, Berkeley: University of California.

Hawking J. (2007), *Travelling to Infinity: My Life with Stephen*, London: Alma Books.

Hawking, S. (1988), *A Brief History of Time. New York: Bantam Books*

Hawking S. (1988), *The Universe in a Nutshell*. New York, Nantam Books.

Hawking S. W., '*In Defence of A Brief History*', Cambridge Review, March 1992, 16.

Hegel G. W. F. (1975). *Lectures on the philosophy of world history. Introduction, reason in history. New York, NY:* Cambridge University Press

Highfield R., Carter P. (1993), *The private lives of Albert Einstein*, London: Faber and Faber.

Huxley T. H., (1893), *Agnosticism, The Popular Science Monthly*, New York: D. Appleton & Company34(46).

Huxley T. H. (1893), *Collected Essays*, Vol. V: Science and Christian Tradition, Macmillan and Co.

Hume D. (1762), *History of England from the Invasion of Julius Caesar to the Accession of Henry VII*, (1 ed.). London: A. Millar in the Strand.

La Mettrie J. O. (2012), *The System of Epicurus*, Cambridge: Cambridge University Press.

Lapouge G. (1899), *L'Aryen: Son Rôle Social*. Paris: Albert Fontemoing ('The Aryan: his Social Role').

Le Goff J. (1985), *Les intellectuels au Moyen Age, Paris: Edition du Seuil.*

Lynn R., Vanhanen T. (2006), *IQ and global inequality*, Augusta, GA: Washington Summit Publishers.

Jefferson Th., (2016), *Notes on the State of Virginia* (1787), London: John Stockdale.

Kaufman A. B., Kaufman J. C. (red. 2018), *Pseudoscience. The Conspiracy Against Science*. Cambridge–London: Cambridge University Press.

Kerr C. (1993), *The idea of a multiversity*, w: *The Uses of the University*, Cambridge: Cambridge University Press.

Kodeks etyki pracownika naukowego (*Code of Ethics for a Researcher*, 2012), Warszawa: PAN.

Kołakowski L. (1994), *Diabeł kłamie również, kiedy mówi prawdę*, w: *Księga pamiątkowa ku czci Leszka Kołakowskiego (The devil also lies when he tells the truth, in: Commemorative book in honour of Leszek Kołakowski)*, Łódź: Wydawnictwo Łódzkie, Wydawnictwo Uniwersytetu Łódzkiego.

Kołakowski L. (1978), *Main Currents of Marxism*, London: Oxford University Press.

Kopernik M (1976), *On the Revolutions of the Heavenly Spheres*, New York: Barnes and Noble.

Kroński T. (1966), Kant, Warszawa: Wiedza Powszechna.

MacIntyre, Alasdair (1984), *After Virtue: A Study in Moral Theory (2nd ed.). Notre Dame, Indiana: University of Notre Dame Press.*

Macmillan M. (1996), *Freud Evaluated. The Completed Arc*, Cambridge, Massachusetts (USA) The MIT Press.

Manuel F. E. (1968), *A portrait of Isaac Newton*, Boston: Harvard university Press.

Merton R. K. (1996), *On Social Structure and Science*, Chicago, University of Chicago Press.

Montesquieu Ch. (1949), *The Spirit of the Laws*, New York: MacMillan.

Newton I. (1999), *The Principia: Mathematical Principles of Natural Philosophy*. Berkeley and Los Angeles: University of California Press.

Pais A. (1991), *Niels Bohr's Times: in physics, philosophy, and polity, Oxford: Clarendon Press.*

Pomeau R. (1969), *La Religion de Voltaire*, Paris: Nizet.

Popper K. R. (1972), *Objective Knowledge: An Evolutionary Approach*, Oxford: Oxford University Press.

Popper K. R. (1974), *The Logic of Scientific Discovery*. London: Hutchinson Publishing Group Ltd.

Popper K. R. (2020), *The Open Society and Its Enemies*, Princeton: Princeton University Press.

Porphyry (1982), *Life of Pythagoras*. Paris: Les Belles Lettre.

Puślecki Z. W. (24), *Sztuczna inteligencja (AI) w modyfikacjach biznesowych i niezauważone przejście od informacji do inwigilacji (Artificial Intelligence (AI) in Modifications Business and Passing Unnoticed from Information to Surveillance)*. Humaniora. Czasopismo Internetowe no. 3 (47)/2024, ss. 101–122.

Reale G. (1989), *Storia della filosofia antica*, v. I: *Dalle origini a Socrate*, Milano: Universita Cattolica Press.

Reale G. (1992), *Storia della filosofia antica*, vol. II: *Platone e Aristotele*, Milano: Universita Cattolica Press.

Reston J. (1995), *Galileo: A Life*, New York: Harper Perennial.

Ripley W. Z., (1899), *The Races of Europe: A Sociological Study*, New York: D. Appleton and Co.

Rorty R. (1989), *Contingency, Irony, and Solidarity*. Cambridge: Cambridge University Press.

Rorty R. (2011), *Intellectual Autobiography*, w: The philosophy of Richard Rorty, Chicago an Salle, Illinois: The Open Court Publishing Company.

Spink J. S. (1960), *French free-thought from Gassendi to Voltaire*. London: University of London Atholne Press.

Szadkowski K. (2015), *Uniwersytet jako dobro wspólne. Podstawy krytycznych badań nad szkolnictwem wyższym* (*The university as a common good. Foundations of critical higher education research*), Warszawa: Wydawnictwo Naukowe PWN.

Szpotański J. (2009), *Cisi i gęgacze (Silent and honking)*, *in: Historia PRL. T. 13, Warszawa: New Media Concept.*

Tischner J. (2018), *Historia filozofii po góralsku* (*History of philosophy in the highlander language*), Kraków: Wydawnictwo Znak.

Tischner J. (2000), *Ksiądz na manowcach (A priest gone astray)*, Kraków: Wydawnictwo Znak.

Tischner J. (2019), *Mądrość człowieka gór (The wisdom of a mountain man)*, Kraków: Wydawnictwo Znak.

Tocqueville A. (2000), *Democracy in America*, Chicago: University of Chicago Press.

Tourner S. (red.), *The Cambridge Companion to Weber*, Cambridge: Cambridge University Press.

Trevelyan G. M., (1944), *English social history – a survey of six centuries – Chaucer to queen Victoria*, Harlow: Longman, Green and Company.

The Magna Charta Universitatum. University World News.

Twardowski K. (2007), *O dostojeństwie Uniwersytetu (On the Dignity of the University)*, Poznań: Zespół ds. Promocji UAM.

Voltaire, (2002), *Philosophical Dictionary*, London: Penguin Books, 2002.

Voltaire (1994), *Philosophical Letters (Letters on the English Nation, Letters on England) (1734)*, New York: Oxford University Press.

Voltaire, (1991), *The Elements of Sir Isaac Newton's Philosophy* (1738; 2nd expanded edition, 1745), Birmingham, AL: Gryphon Editions.

Walicki A. (2014), *Odpowiedź na ankietę „Przeglądu Filozoficznego"* (*Response to the 'Przegląd Filozoficzny' survey*), in: Przegląd Filozoficzny no. 1 (89) 2014.

Wittgestein L. (1961), *Tractatus Logico-Philosophicus*, New York: Humanities Press.

Weber M. (2017), *Economic ethics of world religions*, Cambridge: Cambridge University Press.

Weber M. (1946), *Science as a Vocation*, published as *Wissenschaft als Beruf*, Originally a speech at Munich University, 1918, published in 1919 by Duncker & Humblodt, Munich. From: Max Weber: *Essays in Sociology*, New York: Oxford University Press.

Weber M. (1972), *Wirthschaft und Gesellschaft. Grundriss der verstechend Soziologie, Tübingen*, Verlag J. C. B. Mohr.

Wade N., (2014), *A Troublesome Inheritance: Genes, Race and Human History*, New York: Penguin Random House.

Watson J. D., (1968), The *Double Helix: A Personal Account of the Discovery of the Structure of DNA*, New York: Athenaeum.

White W., Gribbin J. (1995), *Darwin. A Life in Science*, New York: *Simon & Schuster.*

Wittgenstein L. (1967), *Philosophical Investigations*, New York: Fordham University Press.

Wittgenstein L. (1971), *ProtoTractatus – An Early Version of Tractatus Logico-Philosophicus*, Ithaca: Cornell University Press.

Żylicz M. (2020), *Uwagi Zespołu ds. monitorowania wdrażania reformy szkolnictwa wyższego i nauki (Comments of the Team for Monitoring the Implementation of the Higher Education and Science Reform)*, Forum Akademickie no. 2/2020.

Index of names

Studies in Social Sciences, Philosophy and History of Ideas

Edited by Andrzej Rychard

Vol. 1 Józef Niżnik: Twentieth Century Wars in European Memory. 2013.

Vol. 2 Szymon Wróbel: Deferring the Self. 2013.

Vol. 3 Cain Elliott: Fire Backstage. Philip Rieff and the Monastery of Culture. 2013.

Vol. 4 Seweryn Blandzi: Platon und das Problem der Letztbegründung der Metaphysik. Eine historische Einführung. 2014.

Vol. 5 Maria Gołębiewska / Andrzej Leder/ Paul Zawadzki (éds.): L'homme démocratique. Perspectives de recherche. 2014.

Vol. 6 Zeynep Talay-Turner: Philosophy, Literature, and the Dissolution of the Subject. Nietzsche, Musil, Atay. 2014.

Vol. 7 Saidbek Goziev: Mahalla – Traditional Institution in Tajikistan and Civil Society in the West. 2015.

Vol. 8 Andrzej Rychard / Gabriel Motzkin (eds.): The Legacy of Polish Solidarity. Social Activism, Regime Collapse, and the Building of a New Society. 2015.

Vol. 9 Wojciech Klimczyk / Agata Świerzowska (eds.): Music and Genocide. 2015.

Vol. 10 Paweł B. Sztabiński / Henryk Domański / Franciszek Sztabiński (eds.): Hopes and Anxieties in Europe. Six Waves of the European Social Survey. 2015.

Vol. 11 Gavin Rae: Privatising Capital. The Commodification of Poland's Welfare State. 2015.

Vol. 12 Adriana Mica / Jan Winczorek / Rafał Wiśniewski (eds.): Sociologies of Formality and Informality. 2015.

Vol. 13 Henryk Domański: The Polish Middle Class. Translated by Patrycja Poniatowska. 2015.

Vol. 14 Henryk Domański: Prestige. Translated by Patrycja Poniatowska. 2015.

Vol. 15 Cezary Wodziński: Heidegger and the Problem of Evil. Translated into English by Agata Bielik-Robson and Patrick Trompiz. 2016.

Vol. 16 Maria Gołębiewska (ed.): Cultural Normativity. Between Philosophical Apriority and Social Practices. 2017.

Vol. 17 Anita Williams: Psychology and Formalisation. Phenomenology, Ethnomethodology and Statistics. 2017.

Vol. 18 Mikołaj Pawlak: Tying Micro and Macro. 2018.

Vol. 19 Franciszek Sztabiński / Henryk Domański / Paweł B. Sztabiński (eds.): New Uncertainties and Anxieties in Europe. Seven Waves of the European Social Survey. 2018.

Vol. 20 Adriana Mica / Katarzyna M. Wyrzykowska / Rafał Wiśniewski / Iwona Zielińska (eds.): Sociology of the Invisible Hand. 2018.

Studies in Philosophy, Culture and Contemporary Society

Edited by Bogusław Paź

Vol. 21 Jan Felicjan Terelak: Psychology of the Operator of Technical Devices. 2019.

Vol. 22 Dorota Maria Leszczyna: Del idealismo al realismo crítico. La política como realización en José Ortega y Gasset. 2019.

Vol. 23 Zbigniew Drozdowicz: La république des savants. Sans révérence. Traduit du polonais par Catherine Popczyk. 2019.

Vol. 24 Andrzej Waśkiewicz: The Idea of Political Representation and Its Paradoxes. Translated from Polish by Agnieszka Waśkiewicz and Marilyn Burton. 2019.

Vol. 25 Ilona Błocian / Dmitry Prokudin (eds.): Imagination – Art, Science and Social World. 2019.

Vol. 26 Zbigniew Drozdowicz: Faces of the Enlightenment. Philosophical sketches. 2019.

Vol. 27 Włodzimierz Piątkowski: From Medicine to Sociology. Health and Illness in Magdalena Sokołowska's Research Conceptions. 2020.

Vol. 28 Roman Witold Ingarden: Die Mitschriften von den Vorlesungen Martin Heideggers über die Phänomenologische Interpretation von Kants Kritik der reinen Vernunft (Wintersemester 1927/28). Aus dem Manuskript abgeschrieben und das Vorwort verfasst haben: Radosław Kuliniak und Mariusz Pandura. 2020.

Vol. 29 Krzysztof Wielecki / Klaudia Śledzińska (eds.): The Relational Theory of Society. Archerian Studies vol. 2. 2020.

Vol. 30 Zenon Gajdzica / Robin McWilliam / Miloň Potměšil / Guo Ling: Inclusive Education of Learners with Disability – The Theory versus Reality. 2020.

Vol. 31 Jan Felicjan Terelak: Antarctic Winter-Over Syndrome. Narrative Perspective. 2021.

Vol. 32 Nuria Sánchez Madrid / Julia Muñoz Velasco / José Luis Villacañas Berlanga (eds.): El ethos del republicanismo cosmopolita. Perspectivas euroamericanas sobre Kant. 2021.

Vol. 33 Zbigniew Drozdowicz: Academic Culture. Traditions and the Present Days. 2021.

Vol. 34 Jan Felicjan Terelak: Antarctic Isolation as a Mars Habitat Analogue. A Psychological Perspective. 2021.

Vol. 35 Aleksandra Horowska (ed.): The Labyrinths of Leibniz's Philosophy. 2022.

Vol. 36 Bogusław Szuba / Tomasz Drewniak (eds.): Beauty in Architecture. Harmony of Place. 2022.

Vol. 37 Monika Bukowska / Krzysztof Wielecki (eds.): The Transformations of Contemporary Culture and Their Social Consequences. Archerian Studies Vol. 3. 2023.

Vol. 38 Kinga Anna Gajda (ed.): (Non)Commemoration of the Heritage in Eastern Europe. 2024.

Vol. 39 Jan Grzanka: The Forgotten Genius of Physics, a work on Marian Smoluchowski. The Story of Marian Smoluchowski. 2025.

Vol. 40 Bartlomiej Sipiński: Phenomenology of Subjectivity. An Essay on the Dialogue Personalism. 2025.

Vol. 41 Jan Grzanka: Between Physics and Philosophy. The Philosophy of Nature and Philosophy of Physics in the Writings of Marian Smoluchowski. 2025.

Vol. 42 Izabela Bukalska / Rafal Wiśniewski / Magda Ostrowska / Grazyna Pol: Audio Documentary. A Sociological Perspective. 2025.

Vol. 43 Balázs Böcskei / Mariann Fekete / Ádám Nagy / Andrea Szabó: Beyond the Mask: Does a Covid-Generation Exist? 2025.

Vol. 44 Zbigniew Drozdowicz: Academic Life. My Point of View. 2026.

www.peterlang.com

www.ingramcontent.com/pod-product-compliance
Ingram Content Group UK Ltd.
Pitfield, Milton Keynes, MK11 3LW, UK
UKHW041825031026
15587UKWH00002B/576

9 783631 937686